WHAT STUDENTS SAY TO THEMSELVES

INTERNAL DIALOGUE AND SCHOOL SUCCESS

William Watson Purkey

CORWIN PRESS, INC.
A Sage Publications Company
Thousand Oaks, California

For information:

Corwin Press, Inc.
A Sage Publications Company
2455 Teller Road
Thousand Oaks, California 91320
E-mail: order@corwinpress.com

Sage Publications Ltd.
6 Bonhill Street
London EC2A 4PU
United Kingdom

Sage Publications India Pvt. Ltd.
M-32 Market
Greater Kailash I
New Delhi 110 048 India

Printed in the United States of America

Library of Congress Cataloging-in-Publication Data

Purkey, William Watson.
    What students say to themselves: Internal dialogue and
school success / by William Watson Purkey.
        p. cm.
    Includes bibliographical references and index.
    ISBN 0-8039-6694-6 (cloth: acid-free paper)
    ISBN 0-8039-6695-4 (pbk.: acid-free paper)
        1. Academic achievement—Psychological aspects.
    2. Students—Psychology. 3. Self-perception. 4. Motivation
in education. I. Title.
    LB1062.6.P87 1999
    371.8—dc21   99-6722

00 01 02 03 04 05 06 7 6 5 4 3 2 1

Corwin Editorial Assistant:	Julia Parnell
Production Editor:	Denise Santoyo
Editorial Assistant:	Patricia Zeman
Typesetter/Designer:	Lynn Miyata
Cover Designer:	Tracy E. Miller

Contents

Preface

*T*he inner voice of the self has long been recognized by psychotherapists for its vital role in understanding and altering the lives of clients. At the same time, the inner voice of students —*what they say to themselves about themselves*—has been largely overlooked by educators. This book fills two critical gaps in our understanding of the educative process by providing (a) an explanation of how student self-talk is linked with success and failure in school and (b) a description of what educators and schools can do to promote positive and realistic self-talk in students.

Focusing on the internal dialogue of students offers an approach to teaching and learning sharply different from older approaches based on psychoanalysis (emphasizing unconscious motivations), behaviorism (stressing observable behavior), and even from contemporary positions in cognitive psychology (metacognitive processes and information processing) and neuroscience (linking learning to brain functioning), in that it stresses internal dialogue (the whispering self) as the critical agent in academic achievement.

This book is written primarily for teachers and teachers in training, although professional counselors, school psychologists, administrators, and allied personnel will find it useful in understanding the inner world of students. Parents, too, will find *What Students Say to Themselves* a resource in parenting.

A major theme of this book is that the primary task of parents, teachers, counselors, and others is not to provide students with a constant diet of praise, rewards, compliments, and affirmations. The major task is to reduce or eliminate faulty, illogical, negative, and counterproductive student self-talk that results in low self-efficacy, high self-doubt, and persistent self-hatred.

The knowledge base of *What Students Say to Themselves* is drawn from many disciplines. The most valuable of these have been the contributions of psychotherapists such as Aaron Beck, Eric Berne, Albert Ellis, Sidney Jourard, and Donald Meichenbaum. Their research and writing have provided detailed explanations of how internal dialogue influences external behavior and how therapeutic interventions can alter inner conversations. Their contributions provide the scholarly basis for the five chapters of this book.

Chapter 1 presents an overview of the nature and significance of the inner voice of the self. It explains how self-talk is both the product and producer of experience. Chapter 2 provides a wide-lens view of the self by exploring classical, contemporary, and future concepts regarding the nature of self-defining thoughts. The third chapter describes how, when, and where the voice of the self originates. It explains how thought and language are linked, and it emphasizes the importance of the early home environment. Chapter 4 moves from theory to practice by describing what teachers can do to promote positive and realistic self-talk in students. Emphasis is placed on creating and maintaining classrooms without shame, embarrassment, ridicule, and failure. The final chapter defines the entire school as a "signal system" where everything affects, positively or negatively, what students say about themselves to themselves.

Acknowledgments

The contributions of the following reviewers are gratefully acknowledged.

Kerry Robertson
Arbutus Junior Secondary School
Victoria, British Columbia
Canada

Christine H. Watson
Graduate Teaching Assistant
University of Florida
Gainesville, FL

Wesley Hodges
Education Specialist
PRC Education and Evaluation Services
Indianapolis, IN

Mary Ann Sweet
School Counselor
Tomball Elementary
Tomball, TX

Maryellen Towey Shulz
Assistant Professor of Education
Nebraska Wesleyan University
Lincoln, NE

David Sherrill
Associate Professor
University of Hawaii at Manoa
Honolulu, HI

Phillip S. Riner
Professor
Western Washington University
Bellingham, WA

John Novak
Professor of Education
Brock University
St. Catharines, Ontario
Canada

Paula Helen Stanley
Associate Professor
Radford University
Radford, VA

About the Author

William Watson Purkey** is Professor of Counselor Education in the School of Education at the University of North Carolina at Greensboro and cofounder of the International Alliance for Invitational Education. His professional experience includes teaching as a public school teacher, as an Explosive Ordnance Disposal Specialist in the United States Air Force, and as a university professor.

He has been awarded the University of Florida Student Award for Instructor Excellence, the Standard Oil Foundation's Good Teaching Award, and the Outstanding Teacher Award given by Omicron Delta Kappa, National Leadership Honor Society. He is also the recipient of the Distinguished Alumnus Award, given by the School of Education, University of Virginia, the John McGovern Award, presented by the American School Health Association, and the Professional Development Award presented by the American Counseling Association. In 1991, he received The University of North Carolina at Greensboro Alumni Teaching Excellence Award. In 1997, he received the highest award for teaching excellence given by the University of North Carolina System: The Board of Governors Award for Excellence in Teaching.

An active writer, lecturer, and researcher, Dr. Purkey has authored or coauthored over 80 professional articles and nine books, including *Inviting School Success*, now in its third edition, *The Inviting School Treasury*, and *Invitational Counseling: A Self-Concept Approach to Professional Practice*. His interest is in inviting people to realize their potential.

Listening to the Voices of the Inner Self

'Twas whisper'd in heaven, 'twas mutter'd in hell,
An echo caught faintly the sound as it fell.
—Catherine Maria Fanshawe, *Enigma: The Letter H*

Introducing the Voice of the Self

This book is about the inner voice of the self. It addresses the ways students, teachers, and others speak to themselves about who they are and how they fit in their world. It deals with the voices they listen to in their heads, which in turn determine what they do in school. The purpose of this book is to explain and describe what educators and others can do to invite positive and realistic self-talk in students and themselves.

"The whispering self" introduced here has been described in many ways: self-talk, internal dialogue, inner conversations, private speech, verbal mediations, intracommunication, inner voices, per-

1

sonal cognitions, self-statements, and covert conversation, to name a few. But whatever term is used to describe this inner speech, it is clear that self-talk is a vital part of the total thinking process in human consciousness. It arises the moment we think about something, usually with the aid of language we articulate to ourselves.

The way we use language and the language we use give structure to our perceptual world. Although thinking can occur without language, the words we use greatly enhance thinking and influence behavior. When seeking to define ourselves, understand the world, or solve a problem, we hold a private conversation with ourselves. This internal discussion consists of mentally formulating questions and answers.

As an example, listen to Alice's internal dialogue in Lewis Carroll's (1865/1971) *Alice in Wonderland*:

> Dear, dear! How queer everything is today! And yesterday things went on just as usual. I wonder if I've been changed in the night? Let me think: Was I the same when I got up this morning? I almost think I can remember feeling a little different. But if I'm not the same, the next question is 'Who in the world am I?' Ah, that's the puzzle. (pp. 15-16)

Students and teachers talk to themselves about themselves, and this private conversation has a profound impact on what happens in classrooms. Although the primary focus of this book is on student self- talk, what teachers say to themselves is also important and will be addressed at points throughout this book.

There are five propositions embedded in *What Students Say to Themselves* that give it purpose and direction:

1. What parents, educators, and peers think about and how they act toward students influences what students say to themselves.

2. What students say to themselves about themselves determines their success or failure in school.

3. Everybody and everything in and around a school affects what students say to themselves.

4. Altering what students say to themselves involves altering the total school environment and culture.

5. The task of educators is to structure experiences that reduce negative, counterproductive, faulty self-talk while inviting students to define themselves in essentially positive and realistic ways.

Focusing on what students say about themselves to themselves offers an approach to teaching and learning distinctly different from older and better-known pathways to academic achievement based on psychoanalysis (emphasizing unconscious motivations), behaviorism (emphasizing observable behavior) and even from more recent positions of cognitive psychology (emphasizing information processing, metacognitive processes, and higher-order executive capabilities) and neuroscience (linking learning to brain functioning), in that it stresses internal dialogue (the whispering self) as the critical agent in determining success and failure in school.

An example of how distorted and negative self-talk can cripple achievement was provided by a high school student:

Doubting myself has become a way of life for me. When I turn in a paper, I tell myself it's no good. When I ask a girl for a date, I know I'll be turned down. When I apply for college, I know I won't be accepted.

Such negative self-talk often becomes a self-fulfilling prophecy. Students who expect rejection and defeat often become their own worst enemies. They can also become the worst enemies of classmates, teachers, and others.

Distorted and negative self talk by isolated students who don't fit in can have deadly consequences. These consequences can be fueled by parents who are estranged from their children, educators who have double standards in their treatments of students, and by fellow students who are allowed to badger, bully, and taunt those who are different. The responsibility of educators to reduce or eliminate the sources of destructive student self-talk is a theme echoed throughout this book.

Nature of Internal Dialogue

The term *whispering self* is used to describe that part of consciousness that constantly speaks internally, often in innuendo and half-truths. *It is the current self with a voice.* This voice is a critical ingredient in understanding self-concept, self-esteem, and self-efficacy and how they are developed and maintained.

Although self-talk is based on beliefs, it is different in that it has a "here and now" immediate awareness quality. This construct is based on Vygotsky's (1935/1978, 1962) theory concerning the internalization of dialogue as inner speech. Internalized self-talk is thought itself, a theory supported by research (e.g., Butler, 1981; Ellis, 1958, 1962, 1979; Markus & Nurius, 1986; Meichenbaum 1977, 1985). According to Zastrow (1979, 1994), the way to change the self is to change the self's internal dialogue.

Internal dialogue is that part of the human psyche that has been surprisingly neglected by educational researchers and writers. Very little has been written about what people in school say to themselves about themselves and how this constant inner speech regulates how they feel and act. Despite the general recognition of the importance of how people in classrooms think about themselves and their world, this self-talk has received scant attention when compared to standardized test scores or computers in classrooms. Self-talk is one critical domain of human consciousness that remains relatively unexplored, especially as it relates to school achievement.

Even beyond the concerns of academic achievement, the quality of what people in school say to themselves about themselves and their abilities is important in itself, regardless of its connection to academic performance. Positive and realistic self-talk contributes to human dignity and personal efficacy. Here is an example of this shared by a graduate student:

> After twenty years as wife and mother, I was headed for divorce and my first child was leaving home. I found that I had ignored my whispering self for so long, I could no

longer hear it. What a pleasure it has been to discover it again! I reconstructed the self I had been and the messages I received from my inner voice before it was denied. This nurturing of myself from self-talk gave me the courage to go back to school and pursue a new career. I try to listen to the self-talk that encourages me and try not to dwell on the demon side that points out loss and failure. I do not always succeed at this, but it helps to be aware of the choice.

The term *internal dialogue* usually refers to soundless, inner speech that appears the moment something is thought about. (It seems impossible to think without thinking about something!) According to Sokolov (1972), in all instances, people think, remember, and imagine through the use of private conversation. "Inner speech is nothing but speech to oneself, or concealed verbalization, which is instrumental in the logical processing of sensory data, in their realization and comprehension within a definite system of concepts and judgments" (p. 1). This inner speech is a critical component in human consciousness and thought.

As a further example of internal dialogue, turn again to Lewis Carroll's (1865/1971) Alice:

"Come, there's no use in crying like that," said Alice to herself rather sharply, "I advise you to leave off this minute!" She generally gave herself very good advice (though she seldom followed it) and sometimes scolded herself so severely as to bring tears to her eyes, and once she remembered trying to box her own ears for having cheated herself, for this curious child was very fond of pretending to be two people. (p. 10)

This inner voice is "The form-giving, meaning-making part, the narrator who at every waking moment of our lives spins out its account of who we are and what we are doing and why we are doing it" (Anderson, 1990, p. 137). In other words, internal conversations are the interpretative, evaluative thoughts regarding what is happening to us. By listening and gradually making sense of this subtle narration, the self is revealed.

Product and Producer of Experience

The whispering self is the internally audible part of self-relevant experience and is simultaneously the producer and product of human experiences. Because the self is the pervasive product of all life experiences and typically speaks to itself in hushed terms, most people are unaware of its impact on behavior. Yet self-talk allows the individual to organize and control his or her interpretation of the world.

> This inner voice is a powerful force for good and ill in students for it guides and controls overt behavior and academic achievement.

This inner voice is a powerful force for good and ill in students for it guides and controls overt behavior and academic achievement. As Csikszentmihalyi (1990) explained, "People who learn to control inner experience will be able to determine the quality of their lives, which is as close as any of us can come to being happy" (p. 2).

Human existence is a continuous, lifelong process of creating and then responding to inner conversations. Each person seems to have a special recording studio in the brain that records each message that arrives over countless sensory pathways. These recordings are filed in such a way that they serve as a complex message center, constantly receiving, recording, and sending information that speaks to the individual regarding personal value, ability, and courses of action. If this message center provides affirmations of one's personal value and ability and contains elements of hope, respect, and trust, the individual behaves accordingly. When the messages announce personal worthlessness and inability and contain pessimism, contempt, and suspicion, the person loses confidence and efficacy.

Of course, the human mind is not a structure, machine, or computer. It is, as Loftus (1980) points out, an organ or giant gland, an ever-active, pulsing, oxygen-devouring blob of protoplasm that reacts as best it can for its own maintenance, protection, and self-enhancement.

Healthy and Unhealthy Inner Selves

In a relatively healthy personality, as Bandura (1986, 1989, 1994); Seligman (1990); Zimmerman, Bandura, and Martinez-Pons (1992); Schunk (1984, 1989, 1990, 1994); and others have demonstrated, the inner voice can be highly beneficial. It speaks of success, assurance, fulfillment, and provides a large measure of control over feelings and actions.

Scholars who have written about the nature of the self generally agree that individuals who define themselves in essentially positive ways tend to be open to experience, are more willing to disclose their feelings, and face the world with confidence and assurance. *This positive view of self is moderated by realistic assessment.* An example of a positive and realistic self was shared by a student:

> I especially use positive self-talk in situations where I am the one who is broken-up with. Instead of thinking, "I am not good enough" or "I did something wrong," I say to myself, "This wouldn't have worked out because of his issues. It's better that it happened now than wasting my time anymore." Instead of thinking I was rejected, I focus on the opportunities I now have because the relationship did not work out.

Individuals who practice positive and realistic self-talk accept their limitations but also recognize their potentialities.

It seems clear that positive and realistic internal dialogue defuses stress and strengthens resiliency. A student provided an illustration of this:

> After not getting a new job, I became very depressed. I felt that I must have done something or not done something, in order to have not gotten the job. My inner dialogue convinced me that I had "messed up." A good friend pointed out that it was possible that I could have had an excellent interview and still not have gotten the job. Perhaps the person chosen just had more experience. This thought

helped me to look at the situation in a more positive and realistic way.

Growing numbers of research studies have identified the beneficial effects of positive belief systems manifested in self-talk. The research of Scheier and Carver (1993), Seligman (1975, 1990), and others suggests that an optimistic belief system results in better academic performance in the classroom, better performance on the athletic field, and better physical health. Such an upbeat approach to life was portrayed in the delightful book by Clarence Day (1937), *Life with Father*. Father declared he was going to buy a new plot in the cemetery, a plot all for himself. " 'And I'll buy on a corner,' he added triumphantly, 'where I can get out!' Mother looked at him, startled but admiring, and whispered to me, 'I almost believe he could do it' " (pp. 257-258). Father's upbeat, optimistic outlook on life and beyond serves as a beautiful model for living.

As explained by Seligman (1990), Scheier and Carver (1993), and others, when compared with pessimists, optimists are more likely to cope with everyday problems in adaptive ways, take direct action to solve concerns, and tend to grow personally from adversity. In the classroom, students whose inner voices are ones of optimism are far more likely to succeed in school and in life.

> In the classroom, students whose inner voices are ones of optimism are far more likely to succeed in school and in life.

With pessimists, the whispering self discourages feelings of confidence and efficacy. It informs individuals that things are more difficult than they really are while reminding them that they lack the ability to understand or solve problems. This voice speaks of fear, anxiety, and defeat. The research of Ellis (1979), Meichenbaum (1977), Butler (1981), and others established the link between what people say to themselves and how they think, feel, and act.

Internal dialogue has profound effects on individual behavior socially and even biologically (Hartman & Blankstein, 1986). Research by Kiecolt-Glaser and colleagues (Kiecolt-Glaser, Garner, et al., 1984; Kiecolt-Glaser, Ricker, et al., 1984) documents the connections between physical immune functions and self-definitions. Working to alter faulty, irrational, or negative self-talk is an important prerequisite not only for student achievement but for a healthy life as well.

Imagine the internal voice of a student who lacks confidence in herself or himself:

"I can never remember a thing."

"I'm so clumsy."

"I don't think I can do it."

"I never know what to say."

"The teacher doesn't like me."

"I'm a failure."

"My clothes are not as nice as my classmates'."

"I have a hard time learning things."

"I've never been any good at math."

"I'm always lonely."

"I feel so stupid."

"I don't have a nice smile."

"I'm ugly."

"I don't know how to make friends."

"I'm always left out."

"I'm not good at taking tests."

"I never have enough time."

"Everyone is looking at me."

"I'm inferior to other people."

It is difficult if not impossible to achieve much of anything while listening to an inner voice filled with pessimism, self-doubt, and self-hatred.

Now, imagine the inner voice of a successful student. This voice takes a positive and realistic view of one's existence. It accepts reasonable limitations and avoids being overly optimistic.

"I like the way I look."

"I would find that difficult."

"I have a good memory."

"I work well in groups."

"I'm not very good at some things."

"I have lots of friends."

"My feelings are important."

"The teacher likes me."

"I'm a pretty good athlete."

"I like to volunteer for things."

"I can speak in front of the class."

"I make time for what I want to do."

"I can do lots of things."

"I'm smart in school."

"I like the way I'm dressed."

"I enjoy challenges."

It now seems clear that many of the successes and failures that students experience throughout their educational careers are closely connected with their inner voices.

The evidence presented in this book indicates that students' academic failures in basic subjects, as well as the misdirected motivation and lack of commitment often characteristic of the under-achiever, the dropout, the student labeled "at risk," and the socially disabled are in good measure the consequences of, or certainly exacerbated by, their habits of thought. *They tell themselves that they cannot learn, succeed, or assert, even when such things are not objectively true.* They have difficulty because they are incapable of telling themselves that they can succeed. The lack of positive and realistic self-talk establishes limits to performance, and these limits are as "real" as this book.

Research presented by Wiemer and Purkey (1994) suggests that college students tend to be much more supportive and welcoming to others than to themselves and that they tend to be much more unforgiving and hostile to themselves than to others. Support for these findings was provided by Schmidt, Shields, and Ciechalski (1998), who used the biblical injunction to "Love thy neighbor as thyself" (Leviticus 19:18) to suggest that students could be encouraged to "Love thyself as thy neighbor."

An example of negative beliefs is provided by Ken Kesey (1962) in *One Flew Over the Cuckoo's Nest:*

> Man, you're talking like a fool. You mean to tell me that you're gonna sit back and let some old blue-haired woman talk you into being a rabbit?

> Not talk me into it, no. *I was born a rabbit.* Just look at me. I simply need the nurse to make me *happy* with my role.

> You're no damned rabbit. (p. 62)

By accepting oneself as a rabbit, or "dummy," "loser," "nerd," "trouble maker," "wimp," "clumsy," "dweeb," "ugly," or simply "stupid," the whispering self becomes its own defender, regardless of how ultimately self-defeating the defense may be.

Defending the Inner Self

As early as 1965, Zimmerman and Allebrand provided evidence of the ways in which the self defends itself. They demonstrated that poor readers in school lack a sense of personal worth and adequacy to the point at which they actively avoid achievement. For poor readers to study and still fail provides unbearable proof of personal inadequacy. To avoid such proof and to suffer less pain, many students deliberately choose not to try. Their defense against failure is to accept themselves as failures. They tell themselves that it is better *not* to try than to try and be embarrassed or humiliated. By not trying, they maintain control. This strategy of withholding effort to maintain some sense of self-worth has been documented by Berglas (1985), Covington (1992), and others. Glock (1972) stated the situation succinctly: "A negative self-image is its own best defender" (p. 406).

I had a middle-school student who provided an illustration of how the self defends itself. Max was a student who had been badly treated by life, and school had not been a kind place. He had been labeled, sorted, grouped, suspended, expelled, retained, and paddled. These experiences, plus a steady barrage of low or failing grades, resulted in Max wearing a psychological suit of armor.

One could almost imagine hearing the clank, clank, clank as Max walked down the hallway into my classroom. He would enter class encased in his steel fortress, take his seat, and look out the window.

Some teachers considered Max "unmotivated," but he was actually "disinvited" (Purkey & Novak, 1996) and quite purposeful, wearing his suit of psychological armor as protection against a savage world. His negative self-as-student was his best defender. His internal dialogue might sound like this, "The teachers think I'm a delinquent. I will show them just how delinquent I can be."

Research by Kaplan (1980) demonstrated how delinquent behavior can be used to defend the self. After measuring self-esteem and self-reported deviant behavior of students three times over the course of 2 years, Kaplan reported that the more students' self-esteem declined during the first year, the more their deviant behavior increased during the second year. Furthermore, increased deviant behavior among students initially low in self-esteem was associated with an *increase* in their subsequent self-esteem. In sum, low self-esteem preceded delinquent behavior, whereas delinquent behavior raised self-esteem. The student's self-talk might be, "If I can't be the best, I'll be the best at being the worst."

The numerous ways that the whispering self serves as defender were described by one of my graduate students:

> I often talk to myself in three ways. First, I talk out arguments with myself before I present them to other people.

This helps me organize my thoughts and, I hope, appear more polished when I present my thoughts to others. Second, I often "play out" difficult situations to better understand what went on in the interaction. In the privacy of my mind, I can say what I should have said at the time and did not. Sometimes, just pretending to get in a snappy comeback makes me feel better. Finally, I have found that the whispering self can serve almost a therapeutic function. I often "talk out" my problems to myself and allow my thoughts to really formulate as I go along. It's this way, it's almost like talking to a friend.

Scott Adams (1995) captured the process of private speech with his cartoon character Dilbert (Figure 1.1):

In times of need, individuals formulate various courses of action, critique the various options, and finally select what appears to be the most self-enhancing, rejecting the rest. As Dilbert indicates, sometimes the selected choice works, sometimes it doesn't.

Understanding the Voice of the Self

To understand the whispering self, it is helpful to look at what scholars now hold to be true regarding self-theory. This provides a foundation for exploring the voice of the self.

Studying the self and how it speaks to itself has always been a daunting task. As Baldwin and Satir (1987) point out, the self is a very personal matter and can never be known in its entirety. Because the self is culturally bound and primarily implicit, it is difficult to define and measure. Definitive statements about the characteristics, dynamics, origins, and voice of the self remain in the realm of theory. However, an analysis of various explanations and a review of related research provide a host of relatively unexplored avenues to understanding the self and its voice. Among these avenues are *self-efficacy* (Bandura, 1986, 1994) and the *possible self* (Markus & Wurf, 1987). Although contributions differ and variables shift, there are core similarities among various definitions. From these, a composite definition can be synthesized.

As constructed here, the *self* is a complex, dynamic, and organized system of learned beliefs that an individual holds to be true about his or her personal existence. *The whispering self is consciousness manifested in internal dialogue.* It consists of the "I" (subject) and myriad "me's" (object) in continuous inner conversation. When the "I" speaks, the "me's" respond. It is this inner dialogue that provides consistency to the human personality and allows the individual to maintain an internal reference point for antecedents and consequences of perceptions and behaviors.

Embedded in the foregoing definition of self and its voice are five important qualities. The self is (a) organized, (b) dynamic, (c) consistent, (d) modifiable, and (e) learned. These qualities can be illustrated by a simple drawing (Figure 1.2). There are obvious weaknesses in using a drawing to represent the multifaceted, multilayered, highly abstract, and hierarchical constellation called self, yet simple drawings can be helpful in expressing complex ideas.

The Organized Self

Most self-theorists agree that the self has a generally stable quality that is characterized by internal orderliness and harmony. It is not simply a hodgepodge of cognitions and feelings. To picture this internal symmetry, consider Figure 1.2 and imagine that the large spiral represents the organized unity of the "global" self.

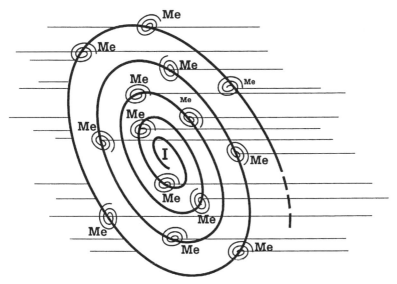

Figure 1.2. The Me-I Constellation

The global self is orchestrated and balanced, centered on the "I," the personal-as-subject. It is this "I" that represents immediate awareness of self-existence. Humans are aware of past, present, and future selves. This future self has been explored by Garcia and Pintrich (1994), Markus and Nurius (1986), and Markus and Wurf (1987). *The "I" is not the content of the self. It is the "here" that experiences the "there."* This "here" and "there" create a relationship between the perceiver and the perceived, all in one person. The relationship gives birth to continuous internal dialogue.

In addition to the "I," the self also contains smaller units. These can be thought of as "subselves" and represent the self-as-object—the various "me's" that are the objects of self-perceptions. Each of the "me" subselves contains its own balance and voice, and each influences, and in turn is influenced by, the global self. As Somerset Maugham (1944) noted in *The Razor's Edge*, more than one individual lives within us, often in uneasy companionship with one another.

The numerous "me" subselves can be roughly divided into "I am" *attributes* (strong, tall, loyal, short, bright, young, friendly, trustworthy, sexy, etc.) and "I am" *categories* (student, husband, mother, Moslem, Jew, American, atheist, athlete, homosexual, veteran, lover, etc.). These perceived attributes and categories usually are linked (good student, loyal American, faithful spouse, responsive therapist) and are positioned in a hierarchical order. This order is critical, for it gives meaning and stability to the global self.

Each person's self contains countless "me's," but not all are equally significant. Some are highly important and are positioned close to the center of the self. Other "me" subselves are less central and are located toward the periphery. Subselves closest to the "I" have the most influence on daily functioning; they speak with greatest authority. At times, they can shout, and the individual "hears" these subselves most clearly. By the same token, subselves farthest away from the "I" have the weakest voices and have diminished influence on perceptions and behavior. For example, listening to the inner voice of "me as a devout Christian" may have vastly greater impact than the voice of "me as a casual golfer."

A personal note may serve as an example. I do not like the taste of spinach. In the event that someone invites me to their home for dinner and serves spinach, it is likely that I will eat what is served. The "me" that dislikes spinach is not nearly as loud an inner voice as the "me" as a somewhat constrained well-mannered person.

Now consider the open areas between the lines of the spiral self in Figure 1.2. They represent the space each person requires to evaluate himself or herself fairly and grow properly. Some people can become so crowded internally with often contradictory "me's" that they experience a sort of sensory overload, continuously adding the voices of new "me's" without letting go of any. When this happens, a person may hear a bedlam of inner voices, behave in confusing and inconsistent ways, and experience difficulty in coping with everyday problems.

An interesting way of understanding the dialogue between the central "I" and countless "me's" is to imagine the "I" as a source of light. Light travels in all directions throughout the universe but is only visible when it encounters something. By analogy, the "I" of personal existence becomes visible only when it is reflected off the various "me's." The "I" cannot see itself directly, any more than the human eye can see itself. The eye knows itself through reflections, just as the self knows itself through life experiences and internal dialogue with countless "me's."

An additional organizational feature of the self is that each subself has its own generally negative or positive value. For example, being a divorced person might be very close to the center of the self, but this could be valued negatively by the experiencing individual. He or she might say to oneself, "Being a divorced person is a highly significant part of my life, and I am constantly aware of it. But I am not comfortable with this fact, and I will hide it from others." Thus, each subself has its own plus or minus voice that contributes to the global self, positively or negatively.

Perceived success and failure tend to generalize throughout the entire self-system. When one "me" is important and highly valued, a failure in that dimension lowers self-evaluations in other, seemingly unrelated, abilities. Conversely, success in a highly valued activity tends to raise self-evaluations in other, apparently unconnected, abilities. This spread-of-effect phenomenon has been documented by Blailiffe (1978), Hattie (1992), and Marsh (1989, 1993), among others.

To illustrate the spread-of-effect phenomenon, return to Figure 1.2 and imagine that each subself (small "me" spiral) is a tiny bell on a mobile. When one bell rings, all others chime in, echoing to some degree the positive or negative note sounded. Consider the self-talk of a student who is an outstanding tennis player. If this student considers himself or herself to be an excellent player and this subself is close to the "I" and highly valued, then consistent success on the tennis court tends to raise self-regard in other areas, such as public speaking or academics. "If I can do well at *this*, I can do well at *that*." However, one important caveat is necessary. A high achiever in any endeavor may become unhappy with success if the achievement is not perceived as valued in one's own eyes and those of significant others. Individuals require positive regard from others as well as from themselves. Only those with clearly atypical personalities could, over time, retain a positive inner voice in the face of consistently negative external evaluations.

One last organizational feature of the self is that each person's self is marvelously unique. Like fingerprints, dental charts, or DNA, no two people think or say identical things about themselves. This uniqueness makes for an infinite variety of human personalities. It also helps explain problems in communication. Because no two people ever think or speak internally to themselves in exactly the same way, it is often difficult for them to agree on what it is they experience. For example, a school counselor will need great sensitivity to understand the perceptual world of a Western Apache student, in which questions display an unnatural curiosity, handshaking violates a person's territory, and talking about trouble increases its chances of occurrence. To the degree that the teacher or counselor can "hear" what the student hears, to that degree can he or she understand, accept, and reflect the feelings of that student.

> To the degree that the teacher or counselor can "hear" what the student hears, to that degree can he or she understand, accept, and reflect the feelings of that student.

The Dynamic Self

Each and every person carries on a continuous internal dialogue. This dynamic activity may be in spoken words or unspoken thoughts and has been going on internally since early childhood, when children learn to whisper to themselves their thoughts and feelings. As Helmstetter (1986) explains,

> At times, our self talk comes in feelings that can't be put into words. At other times it comes in little flashes, flickers of thoughts which never quite catch fire or glow bright enough or last long enough to become ideas, clearly thought out and understood. (p. 36)

It is through this dynamic process that the self is manifested.

To understand the dynamic nature of the self and its voice, picture the global spiral as a sort of personal gyrocompass: a continuously active system of subjective beliefs and thoughts that point to the "true north" of a person's perceived existence. This guidance system is used by the individual to direct actions and take a consistent stance in life. Rather than being viewed as the cause of behavior, the self and its voice are better understood as the gyrocompass of the human personality, providing consistency in personality and direction for behavior.

This was clearly illustrated on an occasion when I invited a former student who had dropped out of school to speak before several hundred educators at a conference on dropout prevention. When the former student arrived, he took one look at the audience and headed for the door. On the way out, he was asked where he was going, and he replied, "I'm a dropout and that's what I'm doing!" The student learned to see himself as a dropout and behaved accordingly.

Bandura (1986, 1994), Seligman (1975, 1990), and others have demonstrated that individuals who tell themselves that they are inefficacious in coping with environmental demands and expectations tend to dwell on their perceived deficiencies and view potential challenges and difficulties as far more difficult than they really are. They defend themselves by negative self-talk that discourages them from facing challenges and difficulties. The biggest challenge in education is not to enhance positive internal dialogue; the biggest challenge is to reduce or ameliorate self-defeating inner conversations. This requires that schools identify, reduce, or eliminate the sources of negative self-talk, recognize negative self-talk whenever it occurs, replace it with positive and realistic inner dialogue, and then practice this new inner voice until it becomes a habit.

> The biggest challenge in education is not to enhance positive internal dialogue; the biggest challenge is to reduce or ameliorate self-defeating inner conversations.

The dynamic nature of the self is evident in the way it can distance the "I" from some subself. For example, a person who has a difficult time jogging might freely admit incompetence to oneself ("If the Lord wanted me to jog he would have given me radial toes.") and downplay the importance of the activity ("Jogging is depressing; I never see a smiling jogger"). Such downplaying of a potential subself (self-as-jogger) takes less effort than excuse making. The process of downplaying the value of a particular activity or reassessing the worth of a certain talent to maintain the integrity of the self has been described by Steele (1988), Steele and Liu (1983), and others. To understand these coping strategies, it is important to recognize that, from each person's perceptual vantage point, any amount of anxiety or distancing involved in a particular threatening action, no matter how painful, self-handicapping, or deceiving, seems preferable to other available avenues of behavior. The reason why this is so is explained by the inner quest for consistency.

The Consistent Self

A singular feature of the self is that it requires consistency in internal dialogue to maintain some degree of homeostatic autonomy. To maintain this consistency, people act in accordance with the ways they have learned to speak to themselves. From a lifetime of studying their own actions and those of others, people acquire expectations about what things fit and what behaviors are appropriate (Calderhead, 1996; Pajares, 1992; Snow, Corno, & Jackson, 1996). All subselves that exist within the global self are positioned to support internal harmony, no matter how inconsistent, self- defeating, or out of line they may appear from an external viewpoint.

If a potentially new inner voice is consistent with those already incorporated into the self, the individual easily accepts and assimilates this fresh voice. However, if the new voice is in opposition to those already incorporated, the person will work to reject it, no matter how positive it might appear to the external observer. People accept and incorporate that which is agreeable and congenial with their present inner voice, and they will work to reject and avoid evidence that is disagreeable and incongruous.

To understand the consistency of self, it is important to consider how things appear from a person's internal point of view. Perceptions of persons with anorexic tendencies illustrate this phenomenon. Clients who have anorexia tell themselves that they are fat in spite of the fact that they are dangerously underweight. To reduce their "I am fat" inner voice, they avoid food, sometimes to the point of starvation.

No matter how illogical, counterproductive, and self-defeating a particular behavior may appear from an external viewpoint, individual behavior has a certain internal logic. Teachers and counselors who can develop the listening skills necessary to "hear" what students are saying privately to themselves, *accept* what students are hearing (acceptance does not mean agreement), and reflect this internal conversation are in a good position to help students alter what they say to themselves about themselves.

Sometimes, the global self consists of contradictory subselves. Yet these various "me's" can coexist happily and may never encounter or challenge one another as long as the individual does not "hear" the contradictions. Once the dissonance is recognized, it has a chance of being resolved. If recognized, but not resolved, the individual is likely to suffer emotional distress.

Behaviors that are incompatible with one's inner voice result in psychological discomfort and anxiety. For example, when speaking at a human sexuality conference, a university infirmary physician commented on the reluctance of some young adults to use contraception although they were having sexual relations. When asked why they did not practice contraception, they explained that if they used contraception, their inner voice would accuse them of *planning* to engage in sexual activity, which they considered "bad" and unacceptable. By not using contraceptive measures when they had sexual intercourse, they could tell themselves that they were swept off their feet in a moment of passion, or at least they were not complicit. Their inner voice tells them that spontaneous sexual activity is far more acceptable than planned sex.

The tendency toward consistency in internal dialogue appears to be an essential feature of the human personality for it provides balance, direction, and stability. If internal dialogue was capricious, the human personality would lack dependability. Under such constructions, daily living would be chaotic and human society impossible.

Teachers and counselors who understand the tendency of the self to maintain consistency do not expect quick changes in students. The whispering self is remarkably conservative and cannot be easily shaped into something more suitable or desirable. Whether a person's internal dialogue is healthy or unhealthy, productive or counterproductive, positive or negative, it strives for consistency and internal logic.

An illustration of how internal logic can conflict with observed behavior is provided in Figure 1.3 by the cartoonist Scott Adams (1995):

One last thought on the consistency of self is that being right about one's beliefs about self has reward value, even if the belief is negative. A student who has just failed an important test might take certain pleasure in stating to oneself: "See, just as I thought! I *told* the teacher I was stupid!" Being right—even about negative feelings about oneself—can be self-satisfying.

A caveat is necessary to avoid picturing internal dialogue as rigid and unchanging. Like the "possible self" described by Markus and Nurius (1986), the whispering self is not well anchored in social experience and does respond to social forces and environmental factors. One of my students provided an illustration of how the whispering self can quickly respond to external factors:

A few weeks ago I had to give an oral presentation in class. That morning I had picked out a nice outfit which I considered to be very "professional." I woke up extra early so that I would have time to get dressed, eat breakfast, and mentally prepare. When I left the house that morning I remember thinking to myself, "Girl, you are ready! You *own* that class! And on top of it all, you look *good*!" With that attitude how could I go wrong?

Things went well and I received excellent reviews from both the professor and my classmates. The interesting thing was that after class I went to the bathroom and happened to catch a glimpse of myself in the mirror. I couldn't believe it!

My hair had fallen, my face was flushed, and my shirt had gotten wrinkled.

"You look like a mess," I thought to myself. If I had looked in the mirror directly before presenting, I would have had great difficulty getting up in front of 30 people. This just goes to show what an important role self-talk can play in our everyday lives.

Fortunately, significant changes in self-talk are possible. Over time and under certain conditions, one's internal dialogue can undergo significant changes. That the whispering self is modifiable is good news for students and their teachers, counselors, and parents.

The Modifiable Self

Inside each reasonably healthy person, new voices appear throughout life while old ones fade away. This continuous change in private conversation creates flexibility in the self and allows for infinite modifiability. A likely explanation for the assimilation of new voices and the expulsion of old ones is the assumption that each person constantly strives to maintain, protect, and enhance the perceived self (Combs, Avila, & Purkey, 1978). This basic assumption is a tremendous "given" for the teacher and counselor, for it means that the self is predisposed toward realizing its potential. The direction this predisposition takes is determined by outer reality as defined by inner voices.

Rather than seeking ways to "motivate" students, the viewpoint presented here is that people are always motivated. There is only one kind of motivation—an internal and continuous incentive that every individual has all the time, in all places, during all activities (Combs et al., 1978). Students may not do what others wish them to do, but this does not mean that they are unmotivated. Educators who accept this assumption can shift their energies away from a "doing to" process of trying to motivate students and toward a "doing with" process of encouraging students to monitor and alter their internal dialogue and choose beneficial directions for this basic drive toward fulfillment.

An example of how the whispering self can be altered by significant others was provided by a student who was serving as president of her high school senior class. When asked how she became interested in politics, she responded that she had never been interested until her junior year. She explained,

> One day I was talking to one of my teachers, idly chatting between classes. We talked about who would make a great senior class president of our high school. After I had named all the "leaders" who had been elected year after year, the teacher asked me a very simple question: "What about you?" I thought to myself, this was the craziest thing I have ever heard! I had never been elected to anything in my life. But that teacher put a bug in my ear. I said to myself, "Why not? " Three weeks later, after I had been elected president of the senior class, the teacher and I laughed about the importance of that conversation and the impact it had on the way I now define myself.

This brings us to the final quality of the whispering self: It is learned.

The Learned Self

Students alter what they say to themselves, for good or ill, in three general ways. The first way is through an extremely traumatic or ecstatic event. All of us have witnessed how an event, such as the tragic loss of a loved one, the joyous arrival of a baby, a high school graduation, an unexpected honor, can have such impact that the very structure of a person's internal dialogue undergoes significant change: "I am a winner," "I am now a widow," "I am now a father," or "I am now a graduate!" The impact of momentous events, such as religious conversion ("I am now saved!") abruptly interrupts the internal balance of the self and tilts it in a new direction. Abrupt events force individuals to reevaluate their internal dialogue.

A sudden physical catastrophe or an irreversible, progressive disability are further examples of traumatic events. Toombs (1994) has described in detail how a physical disability brings on a transformation of the self. The disabled body is closely tied to consciousness, and the whispering physical self speaks with urgency and insistence. According to Toombs, any fundamental change in the body incorporates a profound transformation in internal dialogue.

A second way that internal dialogue is altered is through a professional helping relationship, such as medical treatment, professional counseling, psychotherapy, or spiritual guidance. Many people seek professional help because they have lost the will to challenge the negative and distorted internal voices that dominate their lives. An abundance of empirical research has demonstrated that therapeutic approaches can be beneficial in altering self-debilitating internal dialogue (Beane, 1983, 1990, 1991; Beck, 1976, 1979, 1988; Beck & Emery, 1985; Ellis, 1958, 1979).

An example of the value of professional counseling was provided by my students:

> I have always used self-talk, but it was negative and usually at a very low level of awareness. I did not realize that I was "beating myself up." Through counseling I have come to realize that self-talk can be positively utilized. But I have discovered that positive self-talk is more difficult and has to be done on the conscious level, whereas negative self-talk seems to come naturally. But I am working on it!

Counseling can be a tremendous help in many situations by assisting students in reevaluating and reorganizing their internal conversations.

In addition, medical interventions continue to overcome physical challenges and help individuals lead long and healthy lives. Various forms of medical service, including surgery, drug therapy, and dentistry, both separately and in conjunction with one another, can have powerful effects on what people believe and say to themselves about themselves. As a personal example, I spent most of my life with crooked front teeth which, I told myself, were unsightly. After 3 years of treatment by an excellent orthodontist, my inner voice now encourages me to smile often and widely!

The third and greatest influence on self-talk takes place in everyday experiences. An example is provided by one of Charles Schulz's cartoon characters in *Peanuts*. Linus, Lucy, and Charlie

Brown are shown looking up at cloud formations. Linus says, "That cloud up there looks a little like the profile of Thomas Eakins, the famous painter. And those up there look to me like the map of British Honduras. And that group over there gives me the impression of the stoning of Stephen. . . . I can see the Apostle Paul standing there to one side." Then Lucy says, "Uh-huh. That's very good. What do YOU see in the clouds, Charlie Brown?" And Charlie says, "Well, I was going to say that I saw a ducky and a horsie, but I changed my mind." This is reflection of internal dialogue as only Charles Schulz can reveal it.

Repeated everyday events and interaction with significant others, either positive or negative, have a profound effect on the whispering self. Although most theoretical concepts of the self focus primarily on individual autonomy, recent developments reflect the critical importance of interdependence and relationships with others (Holdstock, 1993, 1994). Asking a student to describe what significant others say about him or her reveals much about what students say to themselves. As early as 1902, C. H. Cooley coined the term "The looking-glass self" to explain that individuals define themselves as they think others define them. As estimated by Csikszentmihalyi (1990), an average person processes about 185 billion bits of information in his or her lifetime. Each and every one of these bits of information is processed and evaluated for its bearing on the self. "Does it threaten our goals, does it support them, or is it neutral?" (p. 39).

> Asking a student to describe what significant others say about him or her reveals much about what the student says to him- or herself.

In concluding this overview of the qualities of the whispering self, it may be helpful to think of the self as a stabilizing lake. The lake is constantly fed by a river of experience that flows into the lake at one end and exits at the other. The river can flow into the lake rapidly or slowly, depending on life experiences, and can provide much or little fresh water. In a healthy personality, the river dependably provides the lake with fresh inner voices, whereas outmoded voices are flushed out of the lake and down the river. When this lifelong process of renewal and development is interrupted and little water is allowed to enter or leave, the lake becomes stagnant and self-talk monotonous. Conversely, if too much water enters the lake, it becomes flooded, unpredictable, and provides too little protection against the vagaries of life. Too many voices are heard, and the person loses self-identity and self-direction.

An aspect of professional helping is to invite students to examine their personal lakes and explore ways to keep them healthy. A healthy self maintains some congruence with the outer world while retaining inner strength and efficacy (Benne, 1984). A healthy self is one that is continuously involved in creating and maintaining new voices that proclaim, "I am able, valuable, responsible, and capable of self-direction."

Summary

This first chapter has presented an introduction to the whispering self. It is this inner speech that verbalizes self-referent experiences.

To provide a foundation for exploring the voice of the self, some major characteristics of the self have been presented. Among these are the following: (a) The self is organized and dynamic, (b) it tends to be conservative but can be modified, and (c) it is learned. Human motivation has been presented as the product of the universal striving toward fulfillment.

Books written in the 1990s by Brinthaupt and Lipka (1994), Greenberg, Rice, and Elliott (1993), Purkey and Novak, (1996), Purkey and Schmidt (1996), Schunk and Zimmerman (1994), among many others, illustrate renewed attention to the self. To place this wellspring of fresh interest in context, it will help to take a look at the whispering self: yesterday, today, and tomorrow.

Developing Concepts
of the Self

When Duty whispers low, Thou must,
The youth replies, I can.
                    —Ralph Waldo Emerson,
            May-Day and Other Pieces, Voluntaries, III

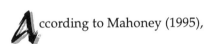 ccording to Mahoney (1995),

> It has been said that the single most important (re) discovery
> of 20th century psychology may well be that of the self, and
> cognitive therapists have joined the rest of the field in ex-
> panding their models and methods to include this elusive
> core dimension of human experience. (p. 11)

Books written in the 1990s by Hattie (1992), Brinthaupt and Lipka
(1994), Purkey and Schmidt (1996), and many others, illustrate this
rediscovery of the self. To understand this renaissance and place the
whispering self in context, it will help to take a historical view and
then to consider some contemporary viewpoints and future projections.

History of the Self

For convenience, this brief history of the self will be compartmentalized into classical history, early-20th-century beliefs, middle-20th-century beliefs, contemporary research, and future directions. Each will be considered in turn.

Classical History and Beliefs About the Self

Throughout human history, there are records of attempts to understand the nature of self. Some have tried through astrological signs, whereas others have used meditation, physical exertion or denial, drugs or religious mysticism. Drawings on cave walls suggest that at some point during the dawn of history, human beings began to give serious thought to their nonphysical, psychological existence: the small, still voice of consciousness.

With the advent of written history, writers would describe this self-awareness in terms of spirit, *aretá, psyche,* or *soul.* Greek philosophers, such as Socrates, Plato, and Aristotle, debated among themselves the conception of an individual's self as a spiritual entity separate from the physical self. This conception formed the foundation for subsequent conceptions of mind-and-body duality. Later, during the Middle Ages, the concept of duality was further developed by theologians, who stressed the immortality and superiority of the soul to the body in which it dwelled.

A turning point in the thinking about the nonphysical self came in 1644, when René Descartes (1644/1912) wrote his *Principles of Philosophy.* Descartes proposed that doubt was a primary tool of disciplined inquiry, yet he could not doubt that he doubted! He reasoned that he could not doubt that he was thinking, therefore he must exist. Although this emphasis on mind and body dualism has been challenged as outdated and dysfunctional, many assumptions of dualism still remain, including the vital role of inner voices of self-awareness.

Other philosophers of the 16th century, among them Spinoza and Leibnitz, added their ideas about the mystery of the nonphysical aspects of individuals. Terms such as *mind, soul, psyche, consciousness, spirit,* and *self* were used interchangeably, with scant regard for invariant vocabulary or scientific experimentation. For the most part, a general state of metaphysical disorganization regarding the self existed well into the present century (and to a large extent continues!). As for *belief,* that concept was exclusively relegated to the realm of religion.

Early-20th-Century Beliefs About the Self

A milestone in the quest for understanding internal processes was the voluminous writings of psychoanalysts such as Sigmund Freud and Carl Jung. Freud (1900/1962, 1923, 1938) gave attention to the self under the concepts of *id, ego,* and *superego.* The concept of ego was given increased attention by his daughter Anna (Freud, 1946), who built a respected place for it in therapy. Specifically, her attention to ego during adolescence provided the foundation for future explorations by theorists such as Erik Erikson (1963, 1968) and James Marcia (1987, 1991). Yet Freudians and neo-Freudians generally hesitated to make the self a primary psychological unit or give it central prominence in their theoretical formulations. In part, this was due to the psychodynamic emphasis on the biological processes in human development, hence the oft-repeated Freudian maxim that "biology is destiny."

Neglect of the self may also have been due to the Freudian emphasis on the unconscious world of the individual. An important contribution of Freud's was his concept that some aspects of experience were well below the surface of consciousness, occurring when there was little or no use of language. In Freud's view, the unconscious is a repository of repressed impulses, savage lusts, and unfulfilled desires. A major emphasis for the Freudians was on the unconscious dimensions of experience, as opposed to conscious processes that involved personal awareness and internal dialogue.

At the turn of the 20th century, when American psychology began to take its place among the other academic disciplines, there was a great deal of interest in self. For example, when William James

(1890) wrote *Principles of Psychology,* his chapter on "The Consciousness of Self" was the longest in the two volumes. James differentiated between the self as knower (the "I") and the self as known (the "me"). He referred to the "I" as *pure ego* and suggested that this component of self is consciousness itself. The "me," on the other hand, is one of the myriad things of which the "I" may be conscious.

James was one of the first to use the term "self-esteem," which he described as a self-feeling of what individuals expect themselves to be and do. Self-esteem may be raised, James argued, either by succeeding in one's endeavors or, in the face of disappointments, by lowering one's sights and giving up certain pretensions.

During the early 20th century, Cooley (1902) used the metaphor of the "looking glass self" to suggest that individuals' self-perceptions are, in part, formed as a result of their perceptions of how other people perceive them. That is, the perceptions and value judgments of others act as mirrors through which individuals view and define their own sense of self. This conception of self brought an emphasis on social interactions and the importance of social comparisons in the development of self to the forefront of psychological, sociological, and philosophical thought.

Thanks to a hectic period of theory building in the early 20th century, followed by strongly held positions on issues, most psychologists rallied around certain systems and organized schools that were characterized by ardent advocacy of their own theories and unrestrained hostility to opposing ones. Freudian psychoanalysts emphasized unconscious motivation; gestaltists believed in the value of insight and stressed the selective perceiver; and behaviorists attempted, with a good deal of success, to cancel out all other schools by claiming that all systems except their own studied consciousness. According to the early behaviorists, only a person's tangible, observable, and measurable behavior was fit for scientific inquiry.

When the smoke cleared, the radical behaviorism of J. B. Watson (1925) carried the day. Psychology was redirected, attention was turned to observable stimuli and responses, and the inner life of the individual was beyond the scope of "scientific" psychology. Self, self-beliefs, self-esteem, self-talk, and self-perception as psychological constructs were pushed into limbo, along with such internal constructs as mind, consciousness, awareness, and will. From the 1920s through the 1940s, the self received scant attention from the behavior-oriented psychologists who dominated American psychology.

Although the decline of interest in the self was encouraged by behavioristic psychologists, all the fault for its neglect cannot be laid at their door. Very little of the literature on the self during those decades was based on disciplined inquiry. Rather, it continued to be philosophic or conceptual in nature, with few studies attempting or reporting empirical findings. The few theorists who advocated the importance of the self weakened their position through neglect of rigorous experimentation and scientific inquiry.

Whatever the cause, emphasis on the self declined as a concern of American psychology and education during the first half of the century. But there were some notable exceptions to this general neglect. George Herbert Mead (1934) made the concept of self a major part of his theoretical writings on the philosophy of transactions with the environment. Mead argued that self results from an interaction between the social process and what Lev Vygotsky (1935/1978, 1962) would later call the "psychological tools" that individuals use to make sense of and share socialization symbols. The primary tool—language—aids individuals in defining their sense of self. Mead also made use of James's "I" and "me" dichotomy to help explain that, "If the 'I' speaks, the 'me' responds." The self is manifested by listening to and making sense of this linguistic exchange.

Other psychologists were instrumental in keeping the study of self alive. Kurt Lewin (1935) viewed the self as a central and relatively permanent organization that gives consistency to the entire personality. Kurt Goldstein (1939) analyzed the process of self-actualization, as contrasted with those actions of the sick organism that must constantly worry about self-preservation. This was a forerunner of the comprehensive works of Abraham Maslow (1954), who was to write so powerfully about self-actualization. Other early contributors included Prescott Lecky (1945), who noted that self-consistency is the primary motivating force in human behavior; Victor Raimy (1948), who introduced measures of self-concept in counseling interviews (and argued that successful psychotherapy is primarily a process of changing the self); and Ernest Hilgard (1949), who presented the thesis that all defense mechanisms imply a self-reference.

Middle-20th-Century Concepts of Self

Coinciding with the zenith of behaviorist influence came what is sometimes referred to as the humanistic revolt in psychology. Dissatisfied with the direction that psychology was taking and apprehensive about what they considered a narrow and passive view of human existence represented by behaviorism, a group of psychologists and psychotherapists called for renewed attention to the internal world of the individual. In concert with existential and phenomenological approaches of the 1950s and 1960s, the humanistic movement was born. As Diggory (1966) noted,

> The fact that the new self psychologists were able to argue substantive matters of learning theory and motivation with the heirs of the behaviorists made the latter pay attention and finally to agree that there might be something to the idea of self after all. (p. 57)

Perhaps the most eloquent and significant voice in this new humanistic movement was that of Carl Rogers (1951, 1959, 1969, 1974), who presented a system of psychotherapy built around the importance of self in human adjustment. Rogers described the self as a social product developing out of interpersonal relationships and striving for consistency. He believed that in every human being, there is a tendency toward self-actualization and growth so long as this is permitted and nurtured by environmental forces. Rogers's approach, using research to support observations, went far towards linking earlier notions about the self with mainstream psychology. In fact, his impact was so powerful and influential that his general approach soon became known as *self theory*.

During the 1960s and 1970s, there was an enthusiastic renewal of interest in the self. The research and writing of Brookover (1959, 1964), Combs et al. (1978), Combs and Snygg (1959), Jourard (1964,

1971), and Purkey (1970), among others, provided a deeper understanding of the dynamics of the self.

> The gap between theory and practice often proved difficult to breach, and many laudable but misguided efforts to nurture self-esteem of the children fell prey to excesses and, ultimately, ridicule.

The influence in schools of the surge of interest in the self-concept was pronounced but uneven. The gap between theory and practice often proved difficult to breach, and many laudable but misguided efforts to nurture self-esteem of the children fell prey to excesses and, ultimately, ridicule. The goal of fostering positive and realistic self-perceptions became mired in controversies over the value of so-called self-esteem education.

One aspect of this renewed attention to self was what was called the human potential movement, which stressed personal growth but sometimes was accompanied by personal excess. As Baldwin (1987) notes, "Unfortunately, proponents of the human potential movement often carried the idea of personal growth to the limits of personal license and failed to develop a disciplined and systematic examination of its assumptions and limitations" (p. 29). This resulted in a backlash against the entire humanistic movement. Once again, interest in the self declined as a viable topic of research.

Late-20th-Century Research on the Self

Interest in the self waned during the 1980s, as psychologists and educators shifted their attention to cognitive processes, information processing, higher-order thinking skills, and simulation of artificial intelligence. This cognitive revolution was heavily influenced by technological advances and the computer, which became the movement's signature metaphor. Much like their humanistically oriented predecessors, the new wave of theorists and researchers emphasized internal, mental events, but this emphasis was primarily on cognitive tasks such as encoding and decoding human thinking, information storage, retrieval, and processing strategies, higher-order thinking, mindful learning, memory processes, and problem solving, rather than on exploring the self and its voice.

This is not to say that interest in the self disappeared completely. In fact, it remained prominent, albeit with a qualitatively different face. In keeping with the "cold cognition" tradition of the cognitive revolution, research on the self maintained a measure of prominence and respectability by adopting a strong quantitative flavor (Greenberg, Rice, & Elliott, 1993; Kaplan, 1980; Meichenbaum, 1977, 1985). Although much of the cognitive approach in exploring consciousness may appear overly mechanistic, its findings have provided exciting insights on the whispering self.

Contemporary Research on the Self

Contemporary emphasis on the self is so pervasive that Graham and Weiner (1996), reviewing the state of knowledge related to theories and principles of human motivation, observed that current research topics, such as self-efficacy, learned helplessness, self-worth, and attributions,

> reflect what is probably the main new direction in the field of motivation—the study of the self. If we add to this list the constructs of self-concept, self-focus, self-handicapping, self-monitoring, and the "self" vocabulary then it is evident that the self is on the verge of dominating the field of motivation. (p. 77)

It is now time to review some of these constructs as they relate to the whispering self.

Self-Efficacy

Perhaps the most prominent self-theorist among contemporary voices is that of Albert Bandura (e.g., 1986, 1989, 1994), who, like Abraham Maslow, is a former behaviorist. In his book *Social Foundations of Thought and Action: A Social Cognitive Theory*, Bandura (1986) wrote that individuals possess beliefs that enable them to exercise a measure of control over their thoughts, feelings, and actions. He noted that "what people think, believe, and feel affects how they behave" (p. 25). Together, these thoughts, beliefs, and feelings compose a self-system; human behavior is the result of the interplay between this system and external forces. Thus, Bandura painted a portrait of human behavior in which the self is the key element.

> The most powerful method of changing cognitions of self-efficacy is performance based.

According to Bandura (1986), how people behave can often be better predicted by their beliefs about their capabilities than by what they are actually capable of accomplishing, although this is not meant to imply that they can accomplish tasks beyond their capabilities simply by believing that they can. The most powerful method of changing cognitions of self-efficacy is performance based. Perceptions of self-efficacy can help determine what individuals do with the knowledge, skills, and talents they possess. More important, self-efficacy beliefs are critical determinants of how well knowledge and skills are acquired in the first place.

Bandura (1989, 1994) also suggested that the process of creating and using self-beliefs is simple enough: Individuals engage in behaviors, interpret the outcomes of their actions, use these interpretations to develop beliefs about their capability to engage in subsequent behaviors in similar domains, and act in concert with the beliefs created. This view of self as a mediating variable in human behavior is consistent with the views of numerous other researchers who have argued that the potent evaluative nature of the self creates a filter through which all new phenomena are interpreted and subsequent behavior mediated. Behavior is not controlled by its consequences (as behaviorists long maintained) so much as it is controlled by personal constructions of its meaning or value in relation to the self.

Social cognitive theory provides a view of human behavior and motivation in which the beliefs that people have about themselves, manifested in inner speech, are key elements in the exercise of control and personal agency. Individuals are viewed as both products and producers of their own environments and of their social systems. A strong sense of self-efficacy enhances human accomplishment and personal well-being in countless ways. People with a strong sense of personal competence approach difficult tasks as challenges to be mastered rather than threats to be avoided. They have greater intrinsic interest and deep engrossment in activities, set challenging goals for themselves and maintain strong commitment to them, and heighten and sustain their efforts in the face of failure. Moreover, they more quickly recover their senses of efficacy after failures or setbacks and attribute failure to insufficient effort or to deficient knowledge and skills. Conversely, people with low self-efficacy may believe that things are tougher than they really are, a belief that fosters stress, depression, and a narrow vision of how best to solve problems. As a result of these influences, self-efficacy beliefs are strong determinants and predictors of the levels of accomplishment that individuals finally attain (Bandura, 1994).

Self-Schemas and Possible Selves

Hazel Markus and associates (Markus & Nurius, 1986; Markus & Wurf, 1987) have presented a perspective on the self that focuses on *self-schemas* and *possible selves*. This perspective presents the view that an individual's self-system is composed on self-schemas, which are defined as "cognitive generalizations about the self, derived from past experience, that organize and guide the processing of self-related information contained in the individual's social experiences" (Markus & Wurf, 1987, p. 64). Markus proposed that one's self comprises the totality of information available to an individual as the result of this total structure when involved in day-to-day activities. People selectively extract from their vast storehouses of self-knowledge the information required to deal with specific events or experiences. The information selected results in the construction of self-schemas that help a person determine the specific stimuli selected for attention, the information to be remembered and incorporated into the self-system, and the inferences and decisions to be made in a particular context. (Seen this way, the concept is similar to Sigmund Freud's description of the executive function of the ego.)

The *possible self* consists of cognitions of the type of person one can become and the things one can accomplish. These cognitions also include the type of person one *fears* becoming. As explained by

Markus, Cross, and Wurf (1990), the possible self is the future-oriented aspect of the whispering self. This inner voice defines what individuals hope they can become, would like to become, or are afraid of becoming. In an earlier view, Erikson (1963) similarly observed that one's self "demands to be synthesized with abandoned and anticipated selves" (p. 160). Because individuals' concepts of their possible selves aid them in selecting information from the self-systems and constructing the self-systems necessary to function adaptively, Markus argued that the possible self provides the essential link between self-concept and motivation.

Self-schemas, then, are parts of the self activated and brought into higher levels of awareness to deal with specific experiences. Because the self includes all available knowledge, an individual must carefully and creatively construct the self-schemas most relevant and appropriate to the experience at hand.

> Individuals are guided by visions of themselves in the future—visions of their possible selves.

Stated another way, self-schemas are conceptions individuals have of themselves in classrooms, on athletic fields, at parties, or with relatives at gatherings. It is the merging of one's self with a particular situation that mediates behavior. Markus suggested that self-schemas are in part constructed from information and strategies that have proven to be effective in past situations of similar nature and reflect significant and enduring personal concerns. They are also constructed to reflect the individual's enduring goals, hopes and aspirations, motives and fears. In constructing self-schemas, individuals are guided by visions of themselves in the future—visions of their possible selves.

Self Theories of the Future

Although it is risky predicting the future of self-research and writing, it seems clear that there is growing awareness among researchers and writers that people respond not to situations but to cognitive and affective representations of these situations. According to Seeman (1988), a phenomenological perspective—the way a person defines one's self and one's world in relation to the self, is absolutely central to understanding human behavior. The growing movement in qualitative research is based largely on the importance of the interpretive aspects of human existence.

John Hattie (1996) has provided an extensive overview of future directions in self-concept research. He maintains that future research will address self-strategies needed to maintain, protect, and enhance self-concept and that future studies will investigate the effects of self-concept on learning. He concludes his predictions regarding future research by stating that much attention will be given to developing valid and reliable self-concept measurement instruments. Among other emerging lines of research that show promise for developing deeper knowledge of the self would be work related to the *shamed self*, the *intuitive self*, and the *shrinking self*.

The shamed self considers the phenomenology of embarrassment. Individuals will go to great lengths to avoid being shamed, and authority figures are quick to use public humiliation and embarrassment to control human behavior. This is particularly true in schools that use shame and ridicule as discipline devices.

Future research on the intuitive self would likely focus on the inner voice that speaks barely above the threshold of awareness. This intuitive self suggests directions, provides feelings of purpose, and takes future events into consideration.

One of the most promising avenues for future research is the shrinking self. The shrinking self involves research on reducing self-awareness in the face of perceived failure, calamity, or stress. *It is the mind's way of telling the whispering self to pipe down.* Baumeister and Boden (1994) present evidence that laboratory experiments as well as clinical insights and everyday experiences support the notion that people sometimes wish to simply forget themselves. This reduction in self-awareness is a limited version of escaping the self totally through self-annihilation. According to Hull and Young (1983), the need to escape the negative aspects of self-awareness seems to be operative among both social drinkers and alcoholics, although alcohol is consumed for a variety of reasons. When faced with threats to one's perceived self, the individual will defend one's self in any manner available, including self-reduction and eventually destruction, as in the form of suicidal behavior.

Shrinking the self is not limited to its negative aspects. There are also positive dimensions, such as peak religious experiences and sheer joy. Csikszentmihalyi (1990) spent years studying people's most joyous and happy experiences. He concluded that a loss of self-awareness is an essential aspect of "flow" experiences. These experiences occur when individuals become totally immersed in an activity to the point where self and its voice temporarily vanish. This loss of self-consciousness does not involve a loss of consciousness of the self. "What slips below the threshold of awareness is the *concept* of self, the information we use to represent to ourselves who we are" (p. 64). The result is unselfconscious confidence.

In addition to emerging self-constructs, many older conceptions are appearing with new names. Jourard's (1971) *self-disclosure* is making a comeback as *self-concealment, self-esteem* is evolving into *self-satisfaction,* and *introspection* is reappearing as *self-focusing.*

The future looks bright for new directions in self research. The central message is that a person's actions are a clear function of how one defines oneself and one's situation in relation to oneself. Although first espoused a half-century ago by Snygg and Combs (1949) and Rogers (1951), this viewpoint is rapidly gaining renewed respectability from a large number of researchers and writers from various perspectives.

Summary

Chapter 2 has provided a brief overview of the history of the self and its voice, from classical approaches to medieval conjectures to, through, and beyond the 20th century. The chapter looked at the self in contemporary research and writing and proposed some future directions for exploration.

Among the most prominent researchers and writers discussed were Carl Rogers and his vision of self-theory, Albert Bandura and his self-efficacy model, and Hazel Markus and associates who proposed the concepts of self-schemas and the possible self. Chapter 3 will explore the development of the whispering self. It will consider the early home and school environments, and their impact—positive or negative—on the whispering self of the developing child.

3

How Internal
Dialogue Develops

Give sorrow words; the grief that does not speak
Whispers the o'er-fraught heart and bids it break.
— Shakespeare, *Macbeth*, IV, iii

As explained in earlier chapters, the whispering self is the always active and evolving personal voice that knows and refers to itself through interactions with the world. From infancy onward, the child derives a biologically driven sense of pleasure from becoming competent in understanding and using the environment. This feeling of competence is a source of satisfaction that appears independent of rewards, punishments, or reinforcements (Deci, 1980). This fits with the concept of human motivation presented in Chapter 1, that every child is *intrinsically* motivated to achieve further and greater control over his or her world by reason of the innate sources of satisfaction that accompany understanding and use of the environment.

Judging by the newborn baby's behavior, it would appear the concept of intrinsic motivation presented by Avila and Purkey

(1966), Combs et al. (1978), and others is correct. Human motivation is the endless struggle to maintain, protect, and enhance the psychological self. Human beings, like all other living organisms, are continuously in search of fulfillment. As described by Helmstetter (1986), the newborn child is a thinking machine that never shuts down. From the moment of birth, the child has been "watching, listening to, sifting, sorting, analyzing, judging, cataloging, and storing" (p. 36) everything that happens. The child is involved in the endless quest for self-identity and self-regard.

The Young Child

The newborn child begins life enclosed in a particular world. Like the air in which the bird flies, the water in which the fish swims, the forest in which the animal lives, this world surrounds the child. The child spends every moment in this world, and it will either maintain, protect, and enhance the child or ignore, abandon, or debase it. The source of the whispering self is whatever is available in the environment— opulence or squalor, acceptance or rejection, beauty or ugliness,

> The source of the whispering self is whatever is available in the environment—opulence or squalor, acceptance or rejection, beauty or ugliness, love or hate, rainbows or gutter water.

love or hate, rainbows or gutter water. All of these provide the basis for the inner pronounced love or hate of one's being.

Immediately, from birth onward, parents and significant others begin an inculturation process so that the child will experience the world in particular ways. Through this process, the child begins to develop a coherent mental organization of the experienced world. Attitudes are expressed and words are attached to things so that the child's perceptions are formed. As suggested by Seligman (1990),

> Your habitual way of explaining bad events, your explanatory style, is more than words you mouth when you fail. It is a habit of thought, learned in childhood and adolescence.

Your explanatory style stems directly from your view of your place in the world—whether you think you are valuable and deserving, or worthless and hopeless. (p. 44)

The most critical "habit of thought" is that of self-awareness.

Emergence of Self-Awareness

Self-awareness is a basic human condition that emerges during the early months of life. Gradually, the infant begins to recognize the presence of significant others, which sets the stage for the beginnings of awareness of self as an independent agent. The child's self-awareness begins to launch forth filaments, like Walt Whitman's (1948) *Noiseless Patient Spider,* to explore the vacant vast surrounding. L'Ecuyer (1992), Mahler (1979), Montmayor and Eisen (1977), Hamachek (1994), and others have documented this development of the self.

During the first year of life, the developing child has learned many things about his or her personal existence. The child has learned "me" and "not me" and to attribute intention to the acts of others. There is now awareness of the major parts of the body and how they relate to each other. Most important, the child begins to sense his or her value as a human being. From this world of continuous experience, the whispering self is formed.

Around the age of 2 years, in a startlingly short time, children begin to discover that everything has a name. At about the same time period, the child begins using the personal pronoun "I," along with "*mine!*" These utterances provide clear indication of the emergence of self-awareness. But long before that, in the first year of life beyond the womb, the whispering self, for better or worse, has been forming. It is this personal voice that defines the child's relationship with his- or herself and the world.

An important way to infer the development of inner speech in children is to ask them to describe themselves. Around the age of 3 to 5 years, they will typically describe themselves by what they do:

"I go to swim class" or "I play with sister." At about the age of 6, they will mention their physical characteristics: "I have brown hair," or "I am a girl." Later, around the age of 9, children will describe personality characteristics, such as "I am friendly," or "I am smart" (Montmayer & Eisen, 1977).

Because the self is not predetermined but is developed as a process of experience, it is remarkably plastic and changeable and possesses an infinite capacity for development. The main force that shapes the self is significant others. Self-evaluations arrive rather directly from the evaluations made of the child by others. "Daddy says I'm stupid" becomes self-talk that whispers, "I'm stupid." Outer voices become inner reality. These evaluations by others are more than words. They are embedded in body language, looks, touch, tone of voice, and other nonverbal messages. It is difficult to overestimate the impact of significant others in the early environment of the child, for in the give and take of countless interactions, children tend to believe what the world believes about them.

An example of how adults can influence how children see themselves was provided by an elementary school teacher:

> One morning, Shannon came into my classroom with her father and announced, "Mama had the baby!" I said to her father, "Congratulations! Is it a boy or a girl?" He answered, "I'll let Shannon tell you all about it. This is her news." With such a thoughtful father, I have the feeling that Shannon and her new little sister will have a very happy life.

Emergence of Language

In Vygotsky's (1935/1978) view, language is a most important tool in development. It is through language that the child learns higher levels of thought. *As children master language, it goes underground as inner speech.* What began as outward verbalization is soon forced by social reprimand and cultural taboo to become internal dialogue. The child learns that calling an adult a "poopie head" or "monkey butt" can bring swift retribution, but thinking these thoughts internally, protected from prying ears, is safe and often satisfying!

Edna St. Vincent Millay (1949) captured the self-talk of a little girl with these words:

> Oh, burdock, and you other dock,
> That have ground coffee for your seeds,
> And lovely long thin daisies, dear—
> She said that you are weeds!
> She said, "Oh, what a fine bouquet!"
> But afterwards I heard her say,
> "She's always dragging in those weeds." (p. 262)

The habits of thought, manifested in the whispering self, are learned early in life. What is laid out are patterns of internal dialogue that influence clouded memories, present interpretations, and future experiences.

Debilitating Early Experiences

As one might expect, parents are the primary caregivers who provide the earliest appraisals of the child's worth. They determine the child's environment by giving or withholding the nourishment of love, affection, security, and physical care. Joan Anglund (1964) described childhood as the happy hour, the tender time of innocence. Unfortunately, many children live in a nightmare. They are psychologically crippled and impoverished by inadequate love and care.

Although sadistic parents do exist, the crippling of children by adults is usually not done on purpose. Few parents want to be failures at raising children, just as few teachers want to fail as teachers or few counselors want to fail as counselors. Yet through lack of knowledge, or insensitivity, or because of a history of their own abuse that they recreate when they raise their own offspring, they cripple their children socially, psychologically, even physically.

In a sad way, the crippling of children might be compared with the ancient Chinese practice of foot binding. In earlier China, mothers would tightly bind their young daughters' feet and keep them bound for years, causing terrible deformity. It was done with the best of intentions. Tiny feet and a mincing walk were considered attractive characteristics for a Chinese woman. In time, the crippled daughter would grow up, marry, and have daughters of her own. The irony: The crippled mother would get out the bandages and cripple her daughters, just as she had been crippled. In generation after generation, like echoes in a canyon, the crippling continued. An old Russian proverb states the problem succinctly: "The little girl who is beaten will beat her doll baby."

Children's capacity to love may be permanently inhibited because important people fail to provide warmth and affection when it is needed most. Their selves are hobbled, distorted, and defeated because participation with the significant people in their lives has given meanings to the self that are pervasively derogatory.

An illustration of how children can think ill of themselves was provided by a social case worker. She reported that when abusing families are reported to authorities, the abused children will typically blame themselves for the parent's abusive behavior. These children tell themselves that they are the cause of their mistreatment.

As a general rule, it can be said that any behavior by significant people that causes a child to despise himself or herself, to feel inadequate, incapable, unworthy, unwanted, unloved, or unable, is crippling. When respect and warmth are missing, when the child's questions go unanswered, when offers to help are rejected, when discipline is based on embarrassment and punishment, when the child's basic rights are abused, there the self is undermined and its voice is filled with self-loathing. Perhaps no greater psychological handicap could exist than that of despising oneself.

> Perhaps no greater psychological handicap could exist than that of despising oneself.

A poignant paradox is that sometimes, the very desire to be a good mother or father will lead the parent to mistake duty for love. The parent thinks, "I'm doing this for your own good" when he or she is excessively critical of the child, pointing out every mistake and picturing it as the child's personal failure. Children of such parents begin to question themselves and their abilities and to define themselves as failures and incompetents.

Other parents, unsure and fearful themselves, become over-protective. They try to shield their children from every danger, real or imagined, near or far. The child is taught that the world is filled with dangers that the child cannot possibly face alone. With the best of intentions, some parents give their children false and misleading descriptions of the world that deeply affect all future learning.

Perhaps the worst affront to the emerging self is to be ignored, to be of little or no consequence. Imagine the unutterable sadness that would develop in a child's mind if no one responded when he or she cried, no one listened when he or she spoke. As Noddings (1984) noted in her book on caring, "To be treated as though one does not exist is a threatening experience, and one has to gather up one's self, one's presence, and place it in a safer, more welcome environment" (p. 19). Often, the most welcoming environment is that of daydreaming, imagination, and fantasy.

So it happens that the early years of life are most critical in forming the child's self-concept. This self is formed from the experiences woven in everyday life, concealed in everyday occurrences, hidden in the deep communications of unspoken feelings. *Gradually, the child becomes the way he or she is treated.*

The Enhancing Home Environment

Successful students, as noted earlier, may generally be characterized as standing high in their own self-regard and as possessing confidence in their abilities to cope successfully in life. Because of the persistent relationship between what students say to themselves and how well or how poorly they function in school, it is helpful to briefly explore the characteristics of the enhancing home environment.

Judging from the available research (Coopersmith, 1967; Deci, 1980), as well as from everyday experience, there seems little room for doubt that parents and other adult caregivers play an extremely vital role in the development of self-regard in their children. Children who grow up in a home environment that encourages them to gain feelings of self-determination and competence tend to develop positive and realistic internal dialogue (Deci, 1980). Their inner voices encourage them to reach out and realize their potentials.

Positive self-talk develops best in a nurturing family environment where individual differences are appreciated, rules are fair, mistakes are accepted, and care is pervasive. Positive self-talk is fostered when children's preferences are acknowledged, even if these preferences cannot be granted. It is vital that parents and other adult caregivers remember that they must have respect, trust, and confidence in their children before their children can develop self-respect, self-trust, and self-confidence.

During these early years, it is the primary adult caregiver, typically the mother, who is in a particularly strategic position. The presence or absence of smiling, kissing, nuzzling, rubbing, tasting, playing, and other nurturing behavior tells the child how wonderful and wanted, or disgusting and unwanted, he or she is. Adult caregivers provide a home base for exploration as a play partner and as a source of comfort when a child is scared, hurt, or distressed.

Together, mothers and fathers, aunts and uncles, grandparents and siblings are critical in molding the child's self-image. An example might be useful here of an exchange between a grandmother and her granddaughter:

Grandmother: Who loves you, Darling?

Granddaughter: Everybody who knows me.

With such an outlook, this little girl's future seems bright.

The classic research that has given us a clear picture of the enhancing home environment is that reported by Coopersmith (1967) in *The Antecedents of Self-Esteem.* Coopersmith identified three basic conditions that lead the child to value and regard himself or herself as a person of worth. These are (a) *parental warmth,* whereby the child senses the love and caring concern of adult caregivers; (b) *respectful treatment,* whereby the child's views are valued and where he or she has a rightful and democratic position in the family;

and (c) *clearly defined limits,* whereby the child comes to know through parents' relatively high demands and expectations that they care about what happens to the child.

It is likely that the emotional climate of the family is as important—or even more so—than economic or social factors. Positive or negative self-statements can exist in a variety of families, including both advantaged and disadvantaged. The critical factor is how the child is consistently treated and how he or she interprets the treatment of significant others. These early findings by Coopersmith (1967) have been supported by more recent studies by Deci (1980) and others.

Entering School

Children come to school for the first time with an inner voice that predisposes them toward achievement or underachievement. Long before the first school bell rings, many children have formed pictures of their value as human beings and of their ability to cope successfully or unsuccessfully with their environment. Like an invisible price tag, the child's internal voice is present wherever he or she goes, influencing whatever is done. For some children, the tag reads, "a fine value," or "an excellent buy," or even "top choice, one of a kind." Unfortunately, others read "soiled," "marked down," or "damaged goods." Each of these tags is a social product given to children by significant people in their lives.

When the invisible price tag is negative, it is probably more destructive than a physical disability, for even the most insensitive parent, teacher, or counselor can usually recognize and take into account a crippling physical disability. A negative inner voice that despises the self is often overlooked because adults fail to take the time and effort it requires to be sensitive to what children say to themselves.

So it happens that a child enters school with a covert voice that constantly murmurs all sorts of ideas about himself or herself and the world. However, in spite of the early influence of the home environment, the school has a great role to play. Next to the home, the school is the single

> Next to the home, the school is the single most important force in determining what students say to themselves about themselves and their abilities.

most important force in determining what students say to themselves about themselves and their abilities.

The School Environment

Traditionally, in North American society, the child is expected to adjust to the school, rather than the school adjusting to the child. To ensure this process, the school is prepared to dispense rewards and punishments, successes and failures, on a massive scale. The child is expected to learn to live in a new environment and to compete for the rewards of obedience and scholarship. Schools stand ready with grades and grade levels, report cards and honor rolls, continuous evaluations and fierce competitions, grouping and labeling, time-out corners, in-school suspension, alternative schools, and a host of other techniques to mold the child to meet the school's expectations.

Because some schools are unable or unwilling to adjust themselves to individual differences among students, children face daily depreciation. Competitive, norm-based evaluations, which ignore vastly different sociocultural backgrounds and individual differences in abilities, often begin in first grade and continue throughout the school experience. It is unlikely that any educational system in the world spends as much time, money, and energy on standardized testing as does the U.S. school system. The result is that many children give up early in school, feeling that with no attempt, there can be little or no humiliation.

Even if a child is performing well in school, he or she can still think, "I'm not smart enough," "I'm not good enough," "I'm not capable enough." This negative self-talk is often planted first by parents and later by teachers who place unrealistic expectations on students. As one boy commented during a therapy session, "It's hard to grow up in a world of perfect people." Simply setting demanding academic standards without recognizing how things seem from the student's side of the desk can lead to lower, not higher, academic performance.

Sadly, there is clear evidence (Burnett, 1993; Harper & Purkey, 1993; Marsh, 1989) that there is a gradual decline in self-evaluations as children move through the educational system. The research of Stipek and MacIver (1989) indicates that students at the junior high school level develop their self-conceptions of ability based on academic performance rather than effort. The student who begins to doubt his or her own intellectual competence is like an athlete betting against his or her own team. The decline in self-evaluation becomes a self-fulfilling prophecy. Like an airplane out of control, declining self-evaluations and declining school performance spiral downward together throughout the adolescent years.

Peer Culture

Among the early and continuing providers of material for the whispering self are peers. Children are everywhere, in day care and on playgrounds, in kindergarten to formal schooling, at parties and sleepovers, and they provide much information for the child. The world of the home is joined with the world of peer relations, creating new information for the development of the inner voice of the emerging student. According to Bandura (1994), peers serve several important functions in influencing the child's self-efficacy. More experienced and competent peers serve as role models. Peers provide comparison data regarding self-efficacy. "Children who regard themselves as socially inefficacious withdraw socially, perceive low acceptance by their peers, and have a low sense of self-worth" (p. 78).

Unfortunately, the chemistry of peer cliques and group cruelty can become deadly. Fellow students can turn on those who don't fit in, calling them names and harassing them in countless vicious ways. Students who are mistreated and estranged from classmates can become violent, as the tragic shooting events in some schools in the late 1990s have proven. A vital role for educators is to build trust with students, have zero tolerance for harassment of any description, and to provide a gentle caring, and nurturing environment for everyone in the school. The concluding chapters will expand on the role of teachers and the school.

As the child interacts more frequently with peers, the influence and expected bias of parents is countermanded by age mates. Unfortunately, childhood peers are not at a level of maturity that allows them to be sensitive to the criticisms and evaluations they place on each other. They do not know that outer voices become inner cognitions, and they are often unaware of the pain they inflict through bullying, taunting, teasing, or simple ignorance. Children can be easily embarrassed and humiliated. As an example, consider the following story shared by a student:

> When I was in sixth grade, I was smitten by the "love bug" for a boy with red hair and freckles. Being very shy, I kept these feelings to myself for a long time. I finally broke down one day and told a girl friend that I was in love. Of course, that bit of information spread like wildfire, and it was only a matter of time that the news got back to my redheaded sweetheart. Meanwhile, I fantasized that he would be swept off his feet upon learning of my love. Several days later, as I was walking down the hallway, I saw my "heart throb" standing in the hallway with a bunch of his friends. They started whispering and giggling among themselves as I walked past. I couldn't help but overhear one boy say to another: "There goes Steve's new girlfriend." Steve's response was "She's not my girlfriend. She's got legs like toothpicks!" It hurts even to this day when I think of the embarrassment and humiliation I felt at that moment. I knew I was a tall skinny kid, but it was the first time I had ever been put down because of it.

The role of peers continues to develop as children move toward and through adolescence. Frequently, the peer group serves as a surrogate for the family, as young people talk to themselves and others about their identities and purposes in life. Sometimes, the peer culture is augmented by the families of friends, particularly boyfriends and girlfriends, and often these families serve almost as second homes.

Everything that happens to a child, and every way it happens, contains messages. These messages can proclaim that the child is able, valuable, and responsible or unable, worthless, and irresponsible. Somerset Maugham (1944), in *The Razor's Edge*, described this process beautifully:

> For men and women are not only themselves; they are also the region in which they were born, the city apartment or the farm in which they learned to walk, the games they played as children, the old wives' tales they overheard, the food they ate, the schools they attended, the sports they followed, the poems they read, and the god they believed in. (p. 2)

The roles of the teacher and school are of particular significance in this inculturation process, and their roles will be explored in Chapters 4 and 5.

Summary

The foregoing overview of the development of the whispering self seems to indicate that homes and schools communicate either a sense of personal adequacy or inadequacy to children. Once a child becomes convinced of his or her inferiority and becomes his or her own worst enemy, then teachers and schools, as well as the student, are in a very difficult, and even dangerous, situation. Fortunately, there are things that teachers and schools can do in encouraging positive and realistic self-talk in students. These will be presented in the next two chapters.

Promoting Positive
and Realistic Self-Talk
in Students

Welcome whisperings are quickly heard.
— Fuller, *The Holy State,* Book 4, Chapter 3

arlier chapters in this book have presented the nature of the whispering self; an overview of the past, present, and future of self theory; and the origins of the self. This chapter focuses on the whispering self of the teacher and what the teacher can do to create an educational environment that promotes positive and realistic self-talk in students.

The task of this chapter is to focus on what teachers say to themselves about themselves, students, and teaching and what they do in the classroom in general. For a host of specific strategies and practical suggestions, the reader is referred to *The Inviting School Treasury* (Purkey & Stanley, 1997). This reference book contains over 110 topics and 600 cross-references explaining how to create and maintain a school environment that intentionally summons every-one in the school to define themselves in positive and realistic ways.

Although academic places, policies, programs, and processes all play important roles in student achievement, it is the teacher who makes the critical difference in student success or failure. Good teaching is a way of being with oneself, one's students, and one's subject. It transcends techniques, skills, or methods. As Palmer (1997) noted: "We teach who we are" (p. 16). Fortunately, the self of the teacher can be employed in such a way that definite positive changes can occur in what students say to themselves, without injury to academic objectives. When students perceive teachers as caring, committed, and curious, they are likely to learn the content of the curriculum.

The way a teacher becomes a beneficial presence in the lives of students rests on two vital factors: (a) the whispering self of the teacher and (b) what the teacher does. Each will be considered in turn.

What Teachers Say to Themselves

To be a beneficial presence in the lives of students, the teacher has the task of achieving mastery over his or her self-talk. In turn, this will result in mastery over consciousness itself. As described by Csikszentmihalyi (1990), consciousness is "intentionally ordered information" (p. 26). Stated another way, the task of teachers is to purposefully monitor negative self-talk, formulate productive internal dialogue, and then practice it until it becomes an automatic part of consciousness.The theoretical position presented in this book is that life experiences evolve into human behavior in the following manner:

Life Experiences
↓
Thought Processes
↓
Beliefs
↓
Whispering Self
↓
Behavior

Although this progression is useful in understanding the flow of development, it is important to remember that the entire process is basically an open system, whereby each step in the flow influences all other steps. The entire process is in a constant state of interaction.

According to Bandura (1986, 1994), Nisbett and Ross (1980), and others, beliefs are the best predictors of the decisions people make and the behaviors they exhibit throughout their lives. These beliefs, jelling into the whispering self and revealing themselves in actions, are critical ingredients in student success or failure in school. As teachers talk to themselves, they create and maintain a world of perceptions regarding themselves, their students, and their subjects. This world of perceptions influences the worlds of students who tend to see themselves as the teacher sees them. A teacher cannot escape the fact that the self-talk of students is within his or her influence.

> A teacher cannot escape the fact that the self-talk of students is within his or her influence.

Whispers About Oneself

Although there is general agreement that teacher self-talk is important in determining how well teachers perform in the classroom, there has been relatively little research conducted on this dimension of the teaching and learning process. Research designed to explore the teacher's whispering self has been scarce. However, inferences can be drawn based on data from related lines of research.

Beutler, Crago, and Arizmendi (1986) reviewed 10 research studies that examined variables in psychotherapy. Nine of these studies supported the importance of therapist well-being. The emotional health of the therapist contributed to positive client outcomes. Similar findings were reported by Wiggins and Giles (1984), who found relationships between counselors' self-esteem and their counseling outcomes. Nutt-Williams and Hill (1996) also reported relationships between therapists' self-talk and therapy process variables.

There has been research on teacher self-efficacy conducted by Ashton and Webb (1986), Moore and Esselman (1992), Ross (1998), and others. These studies indicate that the teacher's sense of efficacy is a powerful construct relating to how much effort they put into their teaching, the goals they establish, and the expectations they hold for their students. A comprehensive review of teachers' efficacy is provided by Tschannen-Moran, Hoy, and Hoy (1998).

What studies indicate is that the *self-as-instrument* concept (Combs et al., 1978, p. 6) is essential to good teaching. Only when teachers possess an inner voice that speaks positively and realistically about themselves and their abilities can they hope to give full attention to the needs of students. Teachers who say to themselves that they are unable, inadequate, and not responsible are in a poor position to teach anything to anyone. Csikszentmihalyi (1990) explained it this way: "How we feel about ourselves, the joy we get from living, ultimately depend on how the mind filters and interprets everyday experiences" (p. 9).

> Teachers who say to themselves that they are unable, inadequate, and not responsible are in a poor position to teach anything to anyone.

Even beyond what happens in the classroom, what teachers say to themselves about themselves is vital in itself. It has value regardless of whether or not it relates to their effectiveness as teachers. The teacher's internal dialogue makes the difference between happiness and unhappiness in the classroom and in life.

There is a relation between what teachers say to themselves about themselves and what they say to themselves about students. Teachers who think good thoughts about themselves tend to evaluate their students more positively. The reverse is true of teachers who rate themselves low on self-concept (Curtis & Altmann, 1977).

Whispers About Students

Purkey and Novak (1996) have presented the idea that teaching is basically "an imaginative act of hope" (p. 1). The task of teachers is to maintain the wellspring of hope, which is caring for oneself. This involves defining themselves in positive and realistic ways and caring for themselves mentally, physically, socially, and spiritually. An expanded list of ways to invite success for oneself, personally and professionally, was provided by Purkey and Stanley (1997).

They present over 1000 suggestions to summon forth the realization of human potential as well as identifying and changing those forces that defeat and destroy potential. A sample of these suggestions include the physical (being a good doctor to yourself), psychological (establishing a personal Fort Knox consisting of special letters, notes, and recognitions received), and intellectual (explore a library and browse through stacks not usually visited). The purpose of these activities is to take good care of oneself in order to take good care of others.

When the teacher thinks positively about students, students tend to respond accordingly. Conversely, when the teacher tells himself or herself that students cannot achieve, then student performance is influenced negatively. This is a form of self-fulfilling prophesy, described in detail by Rosenthal and Jacobson (1968), Insel and Jacobson (1975), and others.

Although no single explanation can cover the fragile and delicate process called teaching, it is becoming increasingly evident that the teacher's internal dialogue about students has the power to influence how students view themselves and how well they learn in school. As Jourard (1968) explained,

> The teacher who turns on the dull student, the coach who elicits a magnificent performance from someone of whom it could not be expected, are people who themselves have an image of the pupils' possibilities; and they were effective in realizing their images. (p. 126)

Positive teacher self-talk about students involves viewing students as able, valuable, and responsible.

Viewing Students as Able

From the moment of birth, human infants are marvelously curious, seeming to obtain a sense of satisfaction and pleasure from exploring, understanding, and mastering their environment. From the earliest years, children rapidly acquire knowledge, which they apply to gain further understanding of their world. Children possess far greater capacities for learning than almost anyone previously had thought possible. Human intelligence is now recognized as dynamic potential, rather than a fixed and static entity, and human potential is seen as filled with possibilities. It is unlikely that anyone has achieved his or her full potential as a human being or as a steward of the national environment.

Students exist not only in their own worlds but also as mental images in the minds of teachers. *Perhaps the most important thing that teachers do is what they do in their minds.* As far back as 1931, John Childs emphasized that if teachers believe that half their students cannot think for themselves, students will behave accordingly.

In sum, when teachers think well of their students and their abilities, students are likely to respond in positive ways. This has been documented by Good (1981), Good and Brophy (1994), Insel and Jacobson (1975), Jones and Panitch (1971), and Pajares (1992), among many others. It is also documented by a personal family experience of mine, when I challenged my young daughter regarding the accuracy of her report of "No homework." In response to the challenge, my daughter stated: "Dad, my teacher says that my word is very important and that you should believe me when I tell you something!" Needless to say, I beat a hasty retreat. Thank goodness for such an encouraging teacher.

Viewing Students as Valuable

Teachers constantly communicate their inner thoughts in their overt behavior. When teachers tell themselves that some students "don't want to learn," "lack the ability," "are unmotivated," "don't care," or "just want to cause trouble," it is likely that their behavior will summon students to respond accordingly. Students live up or down to the teacher's expectations. This seems to be particularly true in working with students identified as disadvantaged.

Martin Haberman (1995) analyzed data based on interviews with more than a thousand teachers and concluded that teachers who are successful in teaching children who live in poverty think and behave differently from those who quit the profession or fail with students. Successful "star" teachers work to find something the student can do, is interested in, and will take ownership of. This is a form of teaching that involves commitment to the notion of the ability, value, and self-directing powers of every student.

According to Haberman (1995), Purkey and Novak (1996), and others, the most effective teachers of disadvantaged students are those who stress the unique value of individual students. Such teachers are sensitive to the fact that children show uneven patterns of achievement and that standardized test scores can be very misleading. Teachers who see each child as a gift commit themselves to confirming their students as being of incomparable and immeasurable value.

How one teacher communicated her value of students was shared by a student:

> When I was in the fifth grade, I was very sick and almost died. My teacher called our home every day. Later, when I returned to school, he helped me catch up. I'll always remember his kindness, and someday I hope to write a book which says, "Dedicated to Mr. Norman Siegel."

Viewing Students as Responsible

Teachers who recognize the limits of their power are more likely to try various ways of teaching. They conduct themselves in ways that remind students of their partnership in the teaching and learning process. As explained by Noddings (1984), "How good *I* can be is partly a function of how *you*—the other—receive and respond to me. Whatever virtue I exercise is completed, fulfilled, in you" (p. 6). By holding students equally responsible for what happens in the classroom, the teacher demonstrates respect for their self-directing abilities.

Research by Deci and Ryan (1987), Kruglanski, Stein, and Ritter (1977), Lepper and Hodell (1989), Matthews (1991), and others indicates that feelings of personal responsibility encourage greater cognitive flexibility and persistence. There is ample evidence (Good & Brophy, 1994, Lepper & Hodell, 1989, Matthews, 1991) that feelings of personal responsibility promote student achievement. When students see change that they have brought about through their own efforts, they are encouraged to see themselves as responsible partners in the teaching and learning process.

Many teachers have discovered the value of a "contract plan" in which students are asked to propose the grade they wish to receive and the work they will satisfactorily perform to earn the grade. When students feel responsible for determining and evaluating their work, they become more interested in their own progress.

Whispers About Teaching and Subject Matter

Throughout history, great teachers have expressed a love for their subjects. The relationship between the teacher and his or her subject matter was beautifully described by Joseph Epstein:

> What all the great teachers appear to have in common is love for their subject, an obvious satisfaction in arousing this love in their students, and an ability to convince them that what they are being taught is deadly serious. (1981, xii)

It is the teacher's commitment to his or her subject that forms students' attitudes toward what is being presented.

Teachers who perceive their subjects as worthwhile and meaningful say to themselves, "This subject is important." "I enjoy teaching this." " I know what I'm talking about." "I love this subject." Conversely, teachers who lack commitment think, "Will this class never end?" "I don't care whether the students learn or not." "I hate teaching this course." "I find this subject boring." If the teacher is bored, it is highly likely that he or she is a boring teacher.

Teachers whose internal dialogue attests to the worthiness of their subjects are most likely to have their passion shared by students. Those who experience meaning, clarity, significance, excitement, and joy in what they teach send a powerful invitation to students to share in these experiences. Their goal is to get students to believe in the intrinsic value of learning something important.

In considering the significance of what teachers think about what they are teaching, it is helpful to also consider what students think about subject matter. Kohn (1994) states that

The question of content is to challenge the assumption that students are indifferent about their schoolwork because they are not sufficiently "motivated" (or, from another point of view, because they simply have low self-esteem). The real problem may be that the work itself is not engaging or relevant. (p. 281)

Students develop healthy inner voices by doing significant things.

What Teachers Can Do

At some point, positive and realistic teacher self-talk is manifested in a consistent behavioral "stance" that communicates to students how much they will learn in the classroom. A successful teacher stance requires being intentional about influencing student self-talk.

Being Intentional

The task of the teacher is to purposefully create for his or her students situations that will invite them to see themselves as able, valuable, and responsible and to behave accordingly (Purkey & Novak, 1996). This guiding image is ultimately assessed through the teacher's intentionality, which is a barometer for successful teaching. Intentionality is what the teacher is about, his or her fundamental project as a helper.

The concept of intentionality in professional helping was introduced by Rollo May (1969), who viewed intentionality as a major variable in successful therapy. May described intentionality as "the structure which gives meaning to experience" (p. 223). He viewed intentionality as the ability to link inner consciousness with overt behavior. By this definition, intentionality "is not to be identified with intentions, but it is the dimension which underlies them; it is man's capacity to have intentions" (p. 224). Defined in this way, intentionality helps to overcome the dichotomy between subject and object. It has value for teachers in monitoring and improving their self-talk and that of their students.

A valuable aspect of intentionality is that it helps teachers to generate multiple choices in a given situation. Ivey (1977), Purkey and Novak (1996), and others have demonstrated that intentional individuals can develop plans, act on many possible opportunities, and evaluate the effects of these actions. Intentionality shapes what teachers hear and see in the classroom.

Combs et al. (1978) illustrate the importance of intentionality with the story of a first grade teacher who had a beautiful head of hair, which she often wore in a ponytail down her back. For the first 3 days of the new school year, she wore her hair this way. On the fourth day she decided to wear it differently and put her hair in a bun on top of her head. By changing her hairstyle, she looked different. One 6-year-old entered the classroom, did not recognize his teacher and, assuming he was in the wrong classroom, left. The principal found the student standing in the hallway, totally lost. Taking the boy by the hand, the principal located the correct class-room and escorted him into class. When the teacher saw the little boy, she quickly approached and said, "Why Joey! It's so good to see you. We wondered where you were and we're glad you're back. We missed you!" The teacher's intentionality was that students are important.

If the teacher's intentionality focused on other factors, her be-havior would have been quite different. For example, if she thought that principals were most important, she might have said: "Boys and girls, this is the *Principal*! Say good morning to the Principal." Or her intentionality might have focused on discipline: "Joey, you're late for class." Or she could have focused on curriculum: "Joey, you have missed much of the lesson." Fortunately, the teacher's intentionality was to focus on the student and his feelings.

Influencing Student Self-Talk

A major assumption of this book is that to change the self, it is necessary to change the self's talk. According to Ellis (1979), Zastrow (1994), and others, faulty, irrational, negative, self-defeating internal dialogue negatively affects teacher interactions with himself or her-self and others. The opposite is also true. Teachers who have positive evaluative thoughts about themselves and others are more likely to be successful in and out of the classroom.

An important task of the teacher is to "give permission" to students to think about what they say to themselves internally. This permission is needed because there is a strong cultural injunction against listening to the voices in one's head. In the eyes of some, talking to oneself is a sure sign of insanity. As explained by Berne (1972),

> Because people who "talk to themselves" are thought to be crazy, nearly everyone has an injunction against listening to the voices in his or her head. This is a faculty which can be quickly recovered, however, if the proper permission is given. Then almost anyone can listen in on his or her own internal dialogues. (p. 274)

The teacher gives permission by encouraging students to listen to and modify their internal dialogue, particularly negative self-talk. When students learn to attend to what they say to themselves, they are in a good position to monitor and alter their inner conversations. Before turning to the process of inviting positive and realistic self-talk in the classroom, it is necessary to again point out the need to avoid instilling negative voices. As stated in Chapter 1, the self is remarkably conservative. Once a student has formed a negative image of oneself and one's abilities, the task of the teacher becomes extremely difficult. Therefore, *the prevention of negative self-talk is a vital element of teaching.*

According to Bandura (1994), it is much easier to undermine student self-efficacy through social persuasion than it is to instill high beliefs. Successful teachers do more than offer flattery, praise, and gratuitous compliments. They structure situations that provide honest, successful experiences. They also avoid placing students in situations where repeated failure is likely. They understand that from the students' point of view, avoiding hurt and failure is more important than obtaining pleasure and success. Where failure is unavoidable, teachers can help students understand that everyone experiences obstacles, setbacks, and defeats in life. This is accomplished by teaching students to reduce or eliminate the debilitating things they say to themselves when they encounter failure.

One popular approach to changing self-talk has been presented by Ellis (1958, 1962, 1979), Maultsby (1975, 1977), Beck (1979), and Zastrow (1994). This approach, called *rational therapy*, is widely used in psychotherapy and counseling to change unwanted emotions and dysfunctional behaviors in clients. In rational therapy, according to Zastrow, working to change negative and dysfunctional self-talk to more rational and positive inner speech is the key psycho-therapeutic agent in making positive and beneficial changes. The process requires that the client works to be aware of internal voices and to challenge those thoughts that are negative and self-defeating.

An important way to confront and challenge negative self-talk is to be on the lookout for tunnel vision (seeing only certain aspects of a situation while ignoring or excluding other relevant informa-tion). Beck (1979, 1988) described faulty irrational thinking and cognitive distortions and recommended remedies.

1. Black or white thinking (dichotomous reasoning). There is only one answer or one way of looking at things. "I am either a success or a failure." In this all-or-none thinking, there is no middle ground. Anything less than perfect is failure. Mistakes are seen as clear evidence of inadequacy. People like me or hate me, they are either friends or enemies. Words associated with this internal dia-logue include "never," "all," "every," "everybody," and "always."

Remedy: Encourage students to think in terms of gray areas. They can be taught to analyze situations in terms of percentages. Things are seldom 100% bad, perhaps 20% or 5%, but not totally bad. Seek to help students see things from a more balanced point of view. Mistakes can be opportunities to learn or as situations that may have been unavoidable.

2. Mental filtering (ignoring or discounting positive factors, while focusing on the negative aspects of a situation). Sometimes, students focus on certain aspects of a circumstance while ignoring all other data. Words associated with mental filtering are "terrible," "awful," "frightful," and "devastating."

Remedy: Ask students to look for evidence of the good things that have happened during the day or to think of the positive aspects of a situation. Consider the many positive things for which they can be thankful.

3. *Mind reading* (thinking that one can know what others are thinking). It is easy to imagine that others are saying things or having thoughts that are simply nonexistent. It is also easy to apply one's own projections into other people's behavior. It is a fantasy to believe one knows what others are thinking.

Remedy: Put it to the test. If a student is concerned with what others are thinking, the student should ask them for verification. As a personal example, one of my colleagues dated a young woman who attended his presentations but she always frowned while he was presenting. This was most disconcerting for my colleague until he learned that she was nearsighted and always frowned when focusing her distance vision. Beck (1985) concluded that people will talk to themselves, and whether relevant or irrelevant, helpful or harmful, this inner voice determines what they will do.

4. *Catastrophizing.* This is an effective way of increasing one's anxiety by focusing on worst possible scenarios. An example is the use of negative self-talk, such as "what if": "What if I run out of teaching materials?" "What if I am called on?" "What if I faint?" "What if the students hate me?" By focusing only on terrible things that could happen, teachers and students blind themselves to separating fact from fantasy.

Remedy: Monitor self-talk to challenge distorted assumptions. Realistically consider the likelihood of a fearful event actually occurring. Check facts.

Fortunately, it is possible to monitor what one says to oneself about oneself and to work at screening out self-debasing and self-destructive inner speech.

Regarding the whispering self, there are good whispers and bad whispers. Compare the two, and imagine the resulting behavior these private statements would generate.

Good Whispers	Bad Whispers
"I feel part of a group of friends."	"I'm not close to anyone."
"I am a friendly person."	"I am too shy to make friends."
"I can make a difference."	"It's just no use."
"This is not working, I'll try something else."	"Nothing works for me."
"I prefer to be polite."	"I *must* be polite at all costs."
"I handle things pretty well."	"I've lost control."
"I sometimes have difficulty in coordination."	"I'm awkward and clumsy."
"I'm making progress."	"I'll never finish."
"I can be creative when I try."	"There's not a creative bone in my body."
"I have a pretty good memory."	"I can never remember names."
"Let's give it a try."	"I know it won't work."
"Good, I'm getting it."	"I'll never get it."
"We've got this opportunity."	"We've got this problem."
"I'm a pretty lucky person."	"I *never* win anything."
"It would be difficult."	"It would be impossible."
"Relax, I'm in control."	"I'm in a complete panic."
"I have a healthy appetite."	"I eat like a horse."
"I sometimes forget where I put my things."	"I'd lose my head if it wasn't tied on."
"I sometimes say the wrong thing."	"I always say the wrong thing."
"I've misplaced my keys."	"I've lost my keys."
"I have power."	"I am powerless."
"I am happy with my life."	"I have a miserable existence."
"Taking part is winning."	"Winning is everything."
"I'll do better next time."	"I'm a failure."
"My feelings are important."	"I should not think of myself."

These "good" and "bad" whispers are only a glimpse of the countless ways in which teachers and students describe themselves to themselves and others.

It is clear that the management of negative self-talk is an important part of the teacher's task. Terms such as "always" can be appropriately restated as "often," "problem" as "situation," "never" as "rarely," "I must" as "I want," "I need" as "I wish." As Meichenbaum (1985) pointed out, shifting terms is not simply a matter of semantics. Rather, it is an *intentional act* on the part of the teacher to help students understand how the words they use can improve or exacerbate classroom learning. Teachers can monitor their own self-talk as a gauge for what is taking place in their thought processes as well as gauging what is taking place in the minds of students.

A practical technique for monitoring and reducing negative self-talk in both the teacher and students is to form a "no-cut contract." The teacher and students formally agree on a four-part pact: (a) I will not put *you* down; (b) you will not put *me* down; (c) you will not put *yourself* down; (d) I will not put *myself* down. This helps to create a positive classroom environment where everyone is on guard against put-downs (negative comments).

In addition to monitoring negative self-talk in the classroom, the teacher can create a climate of optimism and respect. These qualities have high potential for influencing the internal dialogue of students.

Creating a Therapeutic Classroom Atmosphere

The importance of optimism and respect in teaching has been documented in detail by so many writers and researchers that a simple overview of these qualities is sufficient to recognize their value. Detailed information on these qualities may be found in Brinthaupt and Lipka (1994), Burnett (1993), Deci (1980), Harper and Purkey (1993), Helmstetter (1986), Noddings (1984, 1992, 1993), Purkey and Novak (1996), Purkey and Schmidt (1996), Seligman (1990), and Short and Short (1988), among many others.

Optimism

There is clear evidence (Seligman, 1990) that optimism is essential for a good and successful life. According to Seligman, optimists do better in school, succeed more at life's tasks, and even live longer. The teacher's optimism is based on his or her positive and affirming internal dialogue that proclaims "I can make a difference." "I like my students." "These students are bright." "How good these kids are and how much they will learn in my classroom." Compare these self-statements with those of pessimists: "I can't teach these stu-

> Teachers create the classroom environments that make their self-statements come true.

dents." "They don't have the ability." "I'm sure they won't learn a thing in my classroom." "They're unmotivated." Teachers create the classroom environments that make their self-statements come true.

A vivid example of how a teacher can instill negative self-talk was provided by a student:

> I knew the teacher thought I could not handle the course material by the way she treated me different from other kids in the class. Her behavior convinced me that I should drop the class. She treated me like a dummy, so I became a dummy.

Research (Good & Brophy, 1994; Harter, 1992; Matthews, 1991) indicates that teachers tend to treat low and high achievers differently, based on their optimistic or pessimistic views regarding the likelihood of success for these students.

A delightful tribute to optimism and pessimism is offered by Milne (1926) in *Winnie the Pooh*. Listen to the pessimistic self-talk of Eeyore, the old gray donkey, standing by the side of the stream, looking at himself in the water:

> "Pathetic," he said. "That's what it is. Pathetic." He turns and walks slowly down the stream for twenty yards, splashes across it, and walks slowly back on the other side. Then he looks at himself in the water again. "As I thought," he said. "No better from *this* side. But nobody minds. Nobody cares. Pathetic, that's what it is." (p. 70)

Eeyore is always fixated on what is wrong with situations. As a second example, "Good morning, Eeyore," said Pooh. "Good morning, Pooh Bear," said Eeyore gloomily, "if it *is* a good morning, which I doubt" (p. 70).

Compare Eeyore's gloomy outlook on life with that of Pooh Bear, who is free of preconceptions and open to potentialities. When Eeyore loses his tail, he says: "Someone must have taken it . . . how like them." To which Pooh responds, "I, Winnie-The-Pooh, will find your tail for you" (Milne, 1926, p. 44-45). Teachers could do well by applying lessons learned from children's books and fables.

To become an optimist, seek out optimistic role models and practice positive self-talk. As Garcia Marquez (1988) reminds us, human beings "are not born once and for all on the day their mothers gave birth to them, but that life obliges them over and over again to give birth to themselves" (p. 165). Teachers can encourage a rebirth of positive self-talk in students by providing innovative approaches to learning, demonstrating genuine caring for students, and structuring the classroom for productive daily routines. When students see changes they have brought about, they are encouraged to think of themselves and their abilities in a favorable light.

An approach to altering self-talk is offered by Posner, Strike, Hewson, and Gertzog (1982). They reported that for internal dialogue to change, a number of conditions must exist, including the student's awareness that new information presents an anomaly with respect to existing self-beliefs, that this new information should be reconciled with existing beliefs, and that this reconciliation is impossible. This situation inclines the student to reduce tension by talking to himself or herself differently. What this means for the teacher is that to invite students to listen more keenly, learn more deeply, feel more sensitively, the teacher provides situations that create challenges, contrasts, and dissonance in regular patterns of thought.

Respect

According to historical accounts, when Michelangelo went to audition for the task of painting the Sistine Chapel, he carried a note from his teacher. The note read, "This is to introduce Michelangelo the painter who has the ability to do wonderful things if treated with love and respect." Today, as it was in the time of Michelangelo, respect is a critical ingredient for student achievement.

The importance of teachers' respect for students is documented in numerous studies (Amos & Purkey, 1988; Bergman & Gaitskill, 1990; Landried, 1989) involving over 2,000 secondary and post-secondary students. Consistently high correlations were found between teacher respect for students and positive student outcomes.

In their study of teacher's nonverbal behaviors, Arnold and Roach (1989) reported how teachers demonstrated respect for students through such simple daily processes as greetings and leave-takings and starting and ending class on time. Recognizing individual students and being punctual communicate serious academic purpose and respect for students. Arnold and Roach concluded that students in classes taught by these teachers viewed the class as important and, consequently, tended to prepare before coming to class.

Goffin (1989), Purkey and Stanley (1997), Arnold and Roach (1989), and others have offered a series of practical suggestions on ways that teachers can demonstrate respect for students. Among these are eye contact, tone of voice, facial expressions, postures, gestures, dress, verbal messages, taking time to explain difficult material, and displaying a willingness to talk with students outside of class. These and other behaviors communicate consistently high expectations for good conduct, regular attendance, and academic effort. All of these activities have been associated with positive student outcomes.

Teachers who have little respect for students reveal their beliefs by allowing students to skip deadlines and avoid duties and obligations. These teachers grant endless extensions, accept excuses, give good grades with little work and effort, and present challenges as burdens rather than opportunities. Landried (1989) describes how teachers undermine responsibility in students by doing things for students that they could and should do for themselves (for example, picking up their own trash) and by not holding students accountable for respecting others in the classroom.

The heart of respect is appreciation for individual differences. Goffin (1989) offered a series of ways that teachers demonstrate respect for students. Central to these suggestions is sensitivity and appreciation for each student's unique individuality, valuing the rich complexity of groups, and honoring cultural diversity.

Teachers who honor cultural diversity are intentional in portraying various cultural backgrounds in positive ways, responding to the individual rather than labels or stereotypes, and working to overcome the deleterious effects of racism, classism, sexism, homophobia, and other discriminatory practices. *This requires teachers who think within a positive multicultural framework.*

Student self-respect is most likely to be fostered when students are provided with opportunities for real choices, when their views are acknowledged and accepted (acceptance does not mean agreement or acceding), and where honest success experiences are structured.

Structuring Success Experiences

A primary task of the teacher is to structure academic experiences in ways that enhance students' sense of academic efficacy (Zimmerman et al., 1992). The teacher who is success-oriented tends to point out areas of accomplishment rather than focusing on mistakes. Questions a teacher might ask himself or herself when considering success experiences follow:

Do I permit my students opportunities to make mistakes without penalty?

Do I make generally positive comments on written work?

Do I give extra support to students who need special encouragement?

Do I take time to congratulate students on their achievements?

Do I set tasks that are within the abilities of the student?

Do I value student effort as much as student achievement?

Do I seek ways to structure honest success experiences for all students?

Do I value cooperative, collaborative teamwork among students?

Do I hold consistently high expectations for good social behavior?

Students are most likely to learn academic content when the teacher creates a total learning environment that consistently encourages success experiences for all students.

Research related to school success and failure has consistently shown that students' thoughts about themselves as learners improve following success and decline following failure. The psychological devastation on effort, desire, interest, and "motivation" caused by failure has been widely documented (Beane & Lipka, 1986; Glasser, 1997; Kohn, 1994; Purkey & Novak, 1996). There is ample evidence that failure in school is a leading cause of derogatory self-talk.

In addition to reducing or eliminating contrived failure (i.e., the use of the so-called normal bell-shaped curve in grading), teachers can help students deal with honest failures and setbacks that everyone faces in the course of living. What *is* critical, according to Seligman (1990), is what students think to themselves when they encounter failure. The teacher can help students define themselves and their activities in essentially realistic and positive ways. For example, "I did not do well on the SAT, so I will buckle down and prepare myself so that I hit it hard next time. I know I can do better."

An example of how teachers can create successful experiences for students was provided by Clyde Lovelady, a doctoral student and classroom teacher.

Jerry would not take care of my plants most of the year. I asked him to water them, and he told me to do it myself. I begged him to feed my plants and he laughed at me and shook his shaggy red head. One hot spring day, I started to hang three plants next to the window so they could get plenty of sun. Jerry commented on the transfer of these precious plants. "Mr. Lovelady, why are you hanging those ferns next to the window?" Looking at Jerry, I answered in my well-cultivated logic. "Why Jerry, the sun supplies the essence of life. All living creatures, be they human, monkey, plants, or some form of primordial ooze and slime need light and warmth." Jerry rolled his eyes and countered: "But Mr. Lovelady, ferns do better in shade than in strong sunlight. If you leave those ferns there, they will turn yellow. Let me take care of your plants, you don't know how." From then on, Jerry was commissioned "Lord Jerry, Protector of

His Majesty's Plants." My plants did very well during those last few months of school, and so did Jerry.

Students who experience continued honest success in school and whose successes result in approval by significant others over time are likely to develop self-talk that encourages them to put forth the effort, energy, and resources to learn what is being presented in the classroom. Conversely, students who encounter consistent failure and disapproval will move from negative self-talk ("I'm so stupid,") to learned helplessness (Seligman, 1975). Learned helplessness is the giving-up reaction. The student says to himself or herself, "There's nothing I can do to change anything." This lapse into total apathy is often mistaken by educators as lack of motivation.

Summary

This chapter has explored what teachers say to themselves about themselves, students, and teaching. It has tied this internal dialogue to overt teacher behavior that intentionally invites positive and realistic student self-talk. The chapter ended by highlighting the importance of optimism and respect in the teaching and learning process. Chapter 5 will describe what educators can do to positively influence the whispering self of everyone who enters the school.

Creating Schoolwide Strategies to Enhance Positive Self-Talk

Foul whisperings are abroad.

—Shakespeare, *Macbeth*, V.i

*I*t was "one evening deep in June . . . midsummer, to be exact," when the story of "The Mouse and Henry Carson" begins. In this fable of the influence of self-beliefs on academic achievement, Howard Lowry (1961) tells the story of how a mouse ran into the office of the Educational Testing Service and accidentally triggered a delicate point in the apparatus just as the College Entrance Examination Board's data on one Henry Carson was being scored. Henry was an average high school student, unsure of himself and of his abilities. Had it not been for the mouse, Henry's scores would have been average or below average, but the mouse changed all of that, for the scores that emerged from the computer were amazing—800, verbal, 800, quantitative!

When the scores reached Henry's school, word of his academic giftedness quickly spread throughout the building and beyond.

Teachers reevaluated their gross underestimation of this fine lad, counselors trembled at the thought of neglecting such talent, and college admissions officers eagerly recruited Henry for their schools. New worlds opened for Henry. As they opened, he began to grow as a student and as a person. Once he began to be treated differently by the significant people in his life, became aware of his newly discovered academic potential, and began to define himself in light of his previously unsuspected talents, a form of self-fulfilling prophecy took place. Henry gained confidence, began to "put his mind in the way of great things," and became one of the brightest scholars of his generation.

The story of Henry Carson and the fortuitous misstep of the mouse illustrates five propositions of this book, presented in Chapter 1 and paraphrased here:

1. What significant people think about students and how they act toward students influences how students define themselves.

2. How students define themselves in their internal dialogue influences their academic success or failure.

3. Everything the school does and every way things are done influences what students say to themselves.

4. Altering how students define themselves involves altering the total school environment.

5. The task of the school is to structure experiences that reduce crippling self-talk while inviting students to define themselves in essentially positive and realistic ways.

The self-enhancing school is one way to address these propositions.

The Self-Enhancing School

Beane (1994) introduced an "ecological" approach to creating a self-enhancing school. According to Beane, the ecological approach begins with the question of "whether the school as a whole is a self-enhancing place." Beane proceeds to examine "every aspect of the school in light of that question" (p. 81). This model considers the entire school as a self-enhancing place for everyone who enters its doors. Successful schools have one common central focus: students. Everything that is done and every way in which things are done has a direct or indirect impact on what students say to themselves about themselves and their abilities.

Oberg (1987), Strahan (1990), and others have found that educators' decisions are determined by their basic orientation or belief systems regarding themselves, schooling, and their notions of the "good" that frames their personal and instructional decisions. What educators say to themselves about the nature of good teaching and learning and how they think about schools and schooling are thoughts that shape every decision they make as educators. These beliefs create a total school climate and when shared, shape school culture.

To create and maintain a school culture that intentionally focuses on the internal dialogue of students, it is helpful to consider the five areas identified by Purkey and Novak (1996) that are features in every school and that affect students, positively or negatively. In the same way that everyone and everything in hospitals should be a positive influence on patient health, so everyone and everything in the school setting should be a beneficial influence on the self-talk of students. To accomplish this goal, it is useful to focus on five areas: people, places, policies, programs, and processes. These five powerful "P's" compose the educational ecosystem in which individuals continuously interact with themselves and others. A detailed description of the so-called five-P approach in action at the high school level is provided by Hansen and Childs (1998).

The Five Powerful P's

Schools have personalities just like people do. Some are fully alive, whereas others seem brain dead; some are vibrant, some stagnant.

To determine the vitality of any school, it is useful to look through the lens of the five P's.

People

In planning efforts that are designed to have a positive impact on the whispering selves of students, it is important for educators to ask themselves these questions: How do we see ourselves and our students? What are our relationships with one another? And How can we nurture caring relationships that summon forth positive and realistic self-thoughts in students? Answers to these questions point the way to develop a therapeutic school culture.

There appears to be a real hunger in both students and educators for a more caring, gracious, and personalized approach to education, and education can only be personalized by people. No other persons outside the family are in a better position to develop positive and realistic self-talk in students than the people who are employed by schools. These include secretaries, bus drivers, teachers, custodians, food service professionals, principals, supervisors, nurses, aides, librarians, security personnel, and counselors. Although places, policies, programs, and processes all affect the whispering selves of students, it is the people in the process who make the greatest difference. This is reflected in an episode shared by an intercollegiate star athlete:

> There appears to be a real hunger in both students and educators for a more caring, gracious, and personalized approach to education, and education can only be personalized by people.

When I was in elementary school, I hated athletics. It seemed that every recess and every lunchtime was taken up with playing "kickball." One rule in kickball was that if you kicked a "grounder," you were automatically out. I always kicked grounders. Consequently, when it came time to choose up sides, I was always chosen last because I was a grounder kicker. One day, after I had been chosen last, I

kicked my usual grounder. Hearing groans from my team-
mates, I wandered off to think about how bad I was. About
that time, a teacher on playground duty, who had witnessed
my defeat, came over to me, placed a kickball on the ground
in front of me and whispered four words: "Kick under the
ball." At my next turn at bat, I kept saying to myself: "Kick
under the ball, kick *under* the ball." When the ball was rolled
to me, I kicked under the ball and it took off like a rocket! I
ran around the bases as if I were 6 feet off the ground, and
I have loved athletics ever since.

There are no substitutes for caring teachers in influencing what goes
on in students' minds.

Schools that are most successful in encouraging positive student
self-talk are often staffed by faculties who value collegiality. They
work as teams, rather than as groups, and they seek continuous
improvement for their schools. They possess a shared language of
optimism, trust, respect, and intentionality. People in these schools
speak of themselves and their schools in essentially positive ways.
As Sergiovanni (1994) pointed out, these broad-ranging qualities are
based on a different metaphor for schools, one that looks at schools
as therapeutic communities rather than structural organizations.
The school as a whole takes a caring, gracious, and civil approach
to the educative process.

The principal or headmaster is in a particularly advantageous
position to influence the vibrancy of the school. Dworkin, Haney,
Dworkin, and Telschow (1990) investigated the relationships between job stress as related to teaching and stress-induced illness.
They reported that generally the incidence of teacher illness increased as job stress increased. It is interesting, however, that teachers assigned to schools where the principal was seen as supportive
were significantly less likely to report stress-induced illness compared to teachers in schools where the principal was viewed by
teachers as unsupportive. Principals who think of teachers as
unique individuals with particular teaching styles and characteristics tend to encourage mental health. Principals who think of
teachers as objects and functionaries in the system elicit similar
thoughts in teachers: "I'm just a cog in a wheel." "What I think

doesn't matter." "What I do is not important." These self-defeating self-statements are sad ways to define oneself and one's work.

Places

Although people are most important in influencing what students think about themselves, the physical environment of the school is also significant. The landscape, upkeep, aesthetics, and even the sounds and smells of the school can communicate to everyone, "We care about you and we're glad you're here." Regardless of the school's age, extra care can be taken to maintain it as attractively as possible. Room temperature, acoustic qualities, room layouts, lighting, furniture, colors, and displays all contribute to the welcoming feel of the school. Becker (1981) provided evidence that the physical setting of a school has a significant impact on the performance, satisfaction, and happiness of those who work there.

Prolonged exposure to a warm and aesthetically pleasant school environment is likely to have a positive influence on what students and teachers think about themselves. Conversely, a cold and aesthetically ugly environment has the opposite effect. Consider the following:

After hearing a talk on the importance of a welcoming school environment, a teacher sent a note to the principal pointing out that the boy's bathroom on his hall needed some soap, paper towels, and toilet paper. His note was returned to his mailbox with this remark written across the bottom (unsigned) "What do you think this place is—the Hilton?" With such an attitude from the principal, is it any wonder that teachers in the school are so apathetic and students so unruly? Sadly, there are educators that simply expect and accept dirty bathrooms and littered hallways. *There is no excuse for self-imposed squalor in a school.*

Fortunately, research on leadership (Neumann, 1995) suggests that although leaders may not always be able to induce changes in others directly, they may be able to do so indirectly through changing the work setting. By altering people's work environment, new ways of thinking are encouraged. In Neumann's study, faculty members responded less to the leader than to changes they suddenly sensed in the work setting. By enhancing the total physical

environment of the school, educators are in good positions to enhance the self-talk of students and faculty.

Policies

How people in schools see themselves is heavily influenced by
the regulations, rules, codes, orders, mandates, plans, and edicts
created by those in authority. Brophy (1998) noted that lack of choice
in policy making, in rules regarding attendance, or in student evaluations contribute to a less than desirable school climate. Sometimes,
policies are created that, although well-intentioned, place significant pressure on teachers and students. For example, policies that
demand high standards of excellence in grading and promotion are
accompanied by equally high demands to reduce the retention and
dropout rates. According to Weinberg (1989),

> On the already overburdened and meagerly supported
> shoulders of the average classroom teacher is the implicit
> charge to save the children in danger of dropping out while
> at the same time holding to and even upgrading standards
> of excellence for the masses. (p. 73)

Thus, the school demands that students measure up to the standards
of the school, rather than focusing on the best way to help each child,
starting where he or she is at the present time. Academic standards
and expectations are vital to any successful school, and they should
be established and maintained within a circle of respect for the
students.

Regrettably, shame and embarrassment are classroom techniques used to ensure student compliance with rules and expectations. For example, the practice of placing the names of misbehaving
or uncooperative students on chalk boards for public censure is
common and even recommended (Canter & Canter, 1976). Such
tactics hark back to the days of the dunce caps on students or Mao's
Red Guards placing similar caps on their teachers. Few experiences
can do greater damage to what students say to themselves about
themselves than public ridicule.

As explained in Chapter 1, the whispering self is active in its own defense. One way that some students defend themselves against shame and embarrassment is to deliberately ridicule themselves. Dressing outrageously, spiking and coloring their hair, or piercing the body with rings and covering the body with tattoos provide a perfect defense. These students bring their nipple pacifiers to school and say to themselves, "You can't shame me because I am shameless." They have the last mirthless laugh, laughing at themselves. Again, a whispering self can be its own best defender against external assault, although sometimes at great cost.

A further example of how policies can negatively affect how students see themselves was provided by McCaslin and Good (1992). They reported that many of the educational reform policies (e.g., more homework, no so-called social promotions) were established for political rather than educational reasons. Hence, many policies are irrelevant and self-defeating because they are expedient and bow to political demands. Regrettably, in spite of over two decades of interest in reform, educational problems remain as acute as ever. According to McCaslin and Good, "the reforms of the 1980s have not had much effect on American schooling" (p. 4). One possible explanation for this lack of progress is that policies have been imposed that neglect to consider their impact on how people in school define themselves and their situations.

Every school policy, code, rule, and mandate should be examined to ensure that it is fair, inclusive, encouraging, and respectful of everyone in the school. Policies can become the symbolic structures that shape the spirit of the school.

Programs

Schools routinely create and maintain programs as part of their overall service. Programs such as community outreach, parent involvement, peer counseling, special education, and cocurricular and extracurricular activities are all designed to contribute to the goals and objectives of the school.

However, it sometimes happens that well-intentioned programs harm students because they focus on narrow objectives and neglect a wider perspective of human needs and conditions. For example, educational programs that label and group students can negatively affect the positive purposes for which these programs were originally designed (Harper & Purkey, 1993). Some classifications may be necessary in an educational setting, but there is a danger in programs that label, group, and segregate human beings. Early on, Hobbs (1975) warned,

> Categories and labels are powerful instruments for social regulation and control, and they often are employed for obscure, covert or hurtful purposes: to degrade people, to deny them access to opportunity, to exclude "undesirables" whose presence in society in some way offends, disturbs familiar customs, or demands extraordinary efforts. (p. 10)

In reviewing school programs, it is important to ensure that they work for the benefit of everyone. Programs that appear to be ethnocentric, elitist, sexist, or discriminatory require immediate modification or elimination.

Last, there is evidence (Beane, 1990, 1994; McMillan, 1980) that small group programs in and out of the regular classroom for extended periods of time may be useful in encouraging positive self-talk in students, especially in those students who are having trouble with negative feelings about themselves and their abilities. Beane (1990) advocates that the matter of self should be placed squarely into the school curriculum to help students understand themselves and develop optimally.

Processes

Processes are simply the ways things are done in the school. How things are done is equally as important as *what* is done. It is possible for a school to have a winning athletic team as a consequence of unsportsmanlike conduct and victimization of some players or have an all-state band while discouraging many students from participating in a music program. Standardized test scores can be raised in a dishonest fashion, labeling some students and quietly removing them from the testing process. Dropout rates can be lowered by listing former students as "home schooled." Every process found in a school should be evaluated on the basis of its ethical implications.

Sometimes, a process can be so embedded in the life of the school that little thought is given to its positive or negative influence. Darling-Hammond (1997) reported that when schools altered traditional practices so that teachers and students could have extended time together, students showed significantly greater achievement gains. There is no substitute for personalized attention and longer-term relationships between students and teachers. Educators have the responsibility to think systematically about, and construct, learning environments that dependably and imaginatively communicate to students that they are able, valuable, responsible, and capable of behaving accordingly.

An example of a caring and democratic process in action was provided by a student:

> In high school, I had a really important audition for a school play. When I went for the audition, I was so anxious that I rushed my reading and did not feel connected with the material—I felt out of control. The drama teacher thanked me, and I left knowing that I had not done as well as I was capable of doing. I walked out beating myself up with my self-talk: "I'm not good enough," "I'm a bad actor," and so on. I had only been out of the auditorium for a minute when I decided to stop the negative self-talk and take control of the situation. I turned around, went back to the teacher, who was packing her things, and said "I can do better. May I take a few minutes of your time and read again?" The teacher said, "You did seem a little rushed—let's try it again." I did and gave the reading that I knew I was capable of. Thanks to the kindness and understanding of the teacher, I got the part.

When considering the processes involved in schooling, it is vital to look at the symbolic structure of the school—to look beyond the obvious and the apparent to consider the emotional, spiritual, psychological, and sociological contexts of the school. Educators who think in terms of the total gestalt, the powerful five P's, understand the dynamics of how everything works together to create a therapeutic educational environment. Without a guiding model, it is less likely that educators' attempts to enhance the self-evaluations of students would significantly advance. One way of conceptualizing a truly welcoming school environment is to employ the metaphor of the blue and orange cards first developed by Purkey and Stanley (1990).

The Blue and Orange Metaphor

Metaphors allow people to share their thoughts in vivid colors and compelling visions. Studies in semantics (Bateson, 1987; Hayakawa, 1990), cognitive psychology (Beck, 1988; Meichenbaum, 1977), and counseling theory and practice (Gladding, 1992; Grinder & Bandler, 1981) have demonstrated the significance of metaphor in human experience and functioning. Metaphors are not absolutely true or accurate pictures. Rather, they provide a pictorial analogy that communicates the significance of an idea or concept. The metaphor provides a way to think of the total school environment in a fresh way. It presents a model for understanding the symbolic meaning of what really happens in and around school. The blue and orange metaphor represents a highly simplistic version of the symbolic signals and structures that exist between and among everyone who lives and works in a school. Its purpose is to color code everything so that it pervades every facet and function of the school. Here is a brief explanation of blue and orange cards.

In a special collection agency in the brain, there are only two kinds of cards, each containing a bit of information. These are blue cards and orange cards. No matter what information is placed on a card and filed in the brain, the card itself is either blue or orange. What is written on the card represents the content (the lyrics); the color of the card represents the context (the melody).

Blue Cards

These cards carry a message that the person is able, valuable, and responsible. They encourage students to define themselves in beneficial ways. Regardless of content, the context of each blue card summons the student to overcome negative thoughts and realize potentialities. Blue cards encourage an excitement for living and respect for oneself and others. Orange cards are exactly the opposite.

Orange Cards

These cards inform the student that he or she is unable, worthless, and irresponsible. Orange cards warn the student to beware: beware of one's own feelings, of relationships, of life. Orange cards can be so painful that students will do almost anything to escape the hurt. A major power of drugs, alcohol, promiscuous behaviors, and the like is that they turn orange to blue, but the effect is illusionary. They only camouflage and mask the pain of the despising self. In his book, *Lost Boys: Why Our Sons Turn Violent and How We Can Save Them,* Garbarino (1999) points out that boys from middle-class and privileged families may respond to subtle but harmful influences, such as taunting, rejection, and fear, by turning vengeful and violent. One way to help prevent violence by boys, according to Garbarino, is for parents, schools, and others to protect youngsters from dehumanizing influences.

This is what one student wrote about orange cards:

If we are not careful, these little voices we hear in our heads can be deadly. If we get too many orange cards, or too few blue, we begin to think we're worthless failures. Then it's orange alert, eat dirt.

Life or Death

It will be useful to contemplate the deeper meanings of the blue and orange card metaphor. It is not about giving "warm fuzzies," "strokes," forming hug stations, or walking around with IALAC (I Am Lovable And Capable) signboards. Although these exercises may be helpful when used caringly and appropriately, they are insufficient to describe the awesome nature and power of the blue and orange cards. The reason the blue and orange card metaphor is useful is that it serves as a constant reminder that everything in the school counts. The ways in which a phone is answered, the cafeteria food is prepared and presented, a letter is written to parents, a word is spoken, an office is painted, a colleague is treated, a policy is established, or a program is implemented are either blue or orange. Because this is so, those who wish to deal in blue cards must carefully monitor the quality of places, policies, programs, and processes, as well as the nature of every human interaction.

The success resulting from careful monitoring of blue and orange cards was reported by Stanley and Purkey (1994). The Self Concept as Learner Scale (SCAL; Purkey, Cage, & Graves, 1973) was administered to 175 students in the seventh grade and readministered to the same 175 students in the ninth grade. During this same period, the middle school systematically worked to create a more caring, respectful, and optimistic school climate. Results indicated the SCAL scores of the students remained stable over the 2-year period. Their self-concept-as-learner scores did not decline as would have been expected on the basis of the findings of numerous previous studies (Burnett, 1993; Harper & Purkey, 1993; Marsh, 1989; Stipek & MacIver, 1989) that consistently reported dramatic declines in student self-statements through the school years.

Just as scientists from every discipline use metaphors to describe concepts and events for which there are no literal terms, educators can use metaphor in sharing a vision of the welcoming school. The impact of the blue and orange metaphor might provide impetus for people in schools to try new ideas and fresh approaches in influencing the concealed conversations of students.

Blue Leader One

In developing and maintaining self-enhancing schools, the role of the principal or headmaster is critical. School leaders who respect and interact with others, who encourage innovation, and who are committed to quality education are likely to answer positively to the following questions:

Do I work to provide honest success experiences for all students regardless of ability, color, gender, or social class?

Do I work to establish a common language of improvement for the school?

Do I encourage participation in decision making through democratic practices?

Do I give extra support to beginning teachers and others who may need special encouragement?

Do I share information as widely as possible with everyone connected with the school?

Do I rely on "guiding suggestions" rather than autocratic rules to improve the school?

Do I work to ensure that everyone in the school is protected from harassment and harm?

Do I monitor what I say to myself regarding the value, ability, and self-directing powers of everyone in the school?

Although questions are helpful in identifying specific practices, the critical ingredient is to develop a culture of mutual respect, trust, optimism, and intentionality. Creating self-enhancing schools requires that leaders reexamine the manner in which they do business in the school. Improving schools boils down to improving what people in schools say to themselves about themselves, their situations, and their purposes.

Summary

This last chapter has addressed the role of the school in changing and enhancing the whispering selves of students. To do this, the school itself must change by evaluating and enhancing the five powerful P's: people, places, policies, programs, and processes. These five powerful influences were considered in turn. The chapter concluded with the blue and orange metaphor that can be used to examine the symbolic structure of any school.

Conclusion

At some point in the history of education, a myth developed that education has to be either effective *or* humane, efficient *or* caring, and that it is impossible to be both. The sad part about this myth is that it is widely accepted even though there is ample evidence presented in this book to refute it. *There is no contradiction between caring about what students say to themselves and caring about academic content.* Any number of classroom practices can do double duty. A good example of how classroom experiences can be both instructive and caring is provided by Kohn (1994).

> When members of a class meet to make decisions and solve problems they get the self-esteem message that their voices count, they experience a sense of belonging to a community, and they hone their ability to reason and analyze. (p. 279)

The salient point is the attitudinal stance from which the school operates. If schools concentrate on students' internal cognitions, then educational practices revolve around them. If schools focus on excelling, surpassing, or exceeding, then these become most important. The basic issue is what educators believe is important.

Because this book reflects proper regard for the scientific method, perhaps it can end with a simple experiment. Please imagine that you are given an important test on the contents of this book. The test results come back and inform you that your answers were inadequate and your efforts poor. Would this information have an impact on what you say to yourself?

Carl Rogers (1974) wrote the following, which seems to serve as a definitive statement on the whispering self:

> The individual has within himself vast resources for self-understanding, for altering his self-concept, his attitudes, and his self-directed behavior—and these resources can be tapped if only a definable climate of facilitative psychological attitudes can be provided." (p. 115)

Although a facilitative school climate is no guarantee of generally positive internal dialogue of students, an unsuccessful and destructive school environment practically guarantees that students will develop and maintain negative self-talk regarding themselves, their school, and their potential. This book has argued for the utter centrality of the ways students speak to themselves internally, for their voices determine how they behave and what they become in and out of school.

References

Adams, S. (1995). *It's obvious you won't survive by your wits alone.* Kansas City, MO: Universal Press Syndicate.

Anderson, W. T. (1990). *Reality isn't what it used to be.* New York: Harper & Row.

Anglund, J. (1964). *Childhood is a time of innocence.* New York: Harcourt, Brace & World.

Amos, L. W., & Purkey, W. W. (1988). Teacher practices and student satisfaction in dental hygiene programs. *Dental Hygiene, 62*(6), 286-291.

Arnold, V., & Roach, T. (1989). Teaching: A nonverbal communication event. *Business Education Forum, 44*(1), 18-20.

Ashton, P. T., & Webb, R. B. (1986). *Making a difference: Teachers' sense of efficacy and student achievement.* New York: Longman.

Avila, D. L., & Purkey, W. W. (1966). Intrinsic and extrinsic motivation: A regrettable distinction. *Psychology in the Schools, 3,* 206-220.

Baldwin, D. C. (1987). Some philosophical and psychological contributions to the use of self in therapy. In M. Baldwin & V. Satir (Eds.), *The use of self in therapy* (pp. 27-44). New York: Haworth.

Baldwin, M., & Satir, V. (Eds.). (1987). *The use of self in therapy.* New York: Haworth.

Bandura, A. (1986). *Social foundations of thought and action: A social cognitive theory.* Englewood Cliffs, NJ: Prentice Hall.

Bandura, A. (1989). Human agency in social cognitive theory. *American Psychologist, 44,* 1175-1184.

Bandura, A. (1994). Self-efficacy. In V. S. Ramachaudram (Ed.), *Encyclopedia of human behavior* (Vol. 4, pp. 71-81). New York: Academic Press.

Bateson, G. (1987). *Steps to an ecology of mind.* Northvale, NJ: Jason Aronson.

Baumeister, R. F., & Boden, J. M. (1994). Shrinking the self. In T. M. Brinthaupt & R. P. Lipka (Eds.), *Changing the self: Philosophies, techniques, and experience* (pp. 143-160). Albany: State University of New York Press.

Beane, J. A. (1983). Self-concept and self-esteem in the middle level school. *NASSP Bulletin, 67*(463), 63-71.

Beane, J. A. (1990). *Affect in the curriculum: Toward democracy, dignity, and diversity*. New York: Teachers College Press.

Beane, J. A. (1991, September). Sorting out the self-esteem controversy. *Educational Leadership*, 27-29.

Beane, J. A. (1994). Cluttered terrain: The schools' interest in the self. In J. A. Beane & R. P. Lipka, R. P. (Eds.), *Self-concept, self-esteem, and the curriculum* (pp. 69-88). New York: Teachers College Press.

Beane, J. A., & Lipka, R. P. (Eds.). (1994). *Self-concept, self-esteem, and the curriculum*. New York: Teachers College Press.

Beck, A. T. (1976). *Cognitive therapy and emotional disorders*. New York: International University Press.

Beck, A. T. (1979). *Cognitive therapy and emotional disorders*. New York: New American Library.

Beck, A. T. (1988). *Love is never enough*. New York: Harper & Row.

Beck, A. T., & Emery, G. (1985). *Anxiety disorders and phobias: A cognitive perspective*. New York: Basic Books.

Becker, F. D. (1981). *Workspace: Creating environments in organization*. New York: Praeger.

Benne, C. C. (1984). Know thyself. *Professional Psychology: Research and Practice, 15,* 271-283.

Berglas, S. (1985). Self-handicapping and self-handicappers: A cognitive/attributional model of interpersonal self-protective behavior. In R. Hogan & W. H. Jones (Eds.), *Perspectives in personality: Theory, measurement, and interpersonal dynamics* (pp. 235-270). Greenwich, CT: JAI.

Bergman, K., & Gaitskill, T. (1990). Faculty and student perceptions of effective clinical teachers. *Journal of Professional Nursing, 1,* 33-44.

Berne, E. (1972). *What do you say after you say hello? The psychology of human destiny*. New York: Grove.

Beutler, L. E., Crago, M., & Arizmendi, T. G. (1986). Therapist variables in psychotherapy process and outcome. In S. L. Garfield & A. E. Bergin (Eds.), *Handbook of psychotherapy and behavior change* (3rd. ed., pp. 257-310). New York: John Wiley.

Blailiffe, B. (1978, March) *The significance of the self-concept in the knowledge society.* Paper presented at the meeting of the Self-Concept Symposium, Boston, MA.

Brinthaupt, T. M., & Lipka, R. P. (1994). (Eds.). *Changing the self: Philosophies, techniques, and experiences.* Albany: State University of New York Press.

Brookover, W. B. (1959). A social-psychological conception of classroom learning. *School and society, 87,* 84-87.

Brookover, W. B. (1964). Self-concept of ability and school achievement. *Sociology of Education, 37,* 271-278.

Brophy, J. (1998). *Motivating students to learn.* Boston: McGraw-Hill

Burnett, P. (1993, March). *Self-concept, self-esteem, and self-talk: Implications for counseling children.* Presentation at the American Counseling Association Conference, Atlanta, GA.

Butler, P. E. (1981). *Talking to yourself: Learning the language of self-support.* San Francisco: Harper & Row.

Calderhead, J. (1996). Teachers' beliefs and knowledge. In D. C. Berliner & R. C. Calfee (Eds.), *Handbook of educational psychology* (pp. 709-725). New York: Macmillan.

Canter, L., & Canter, M. (1976). *Assertive discipline: A take-charge approach for today's educator.* Santa Monica, CA: Canter.

Carroll, L. (1971). *Alice in Wonderland.* New York: Norton. (Originally published in 1865).

Childs, J. L. (1931). *Education and the philosophy of experimentalism.* New York: Century.

Combs, A. W., Avila, D. L., & Purkey, W. W. (1978). *Helping relationships: Basic concepts for the helping professions* (2nd. ed.). Boston: Allyn & Bacon.

Combs, A. W., & Snygg, D. (1959). *Individual behavior* (2nd. ed.). New York: Harper & Row.

Cooley, C. H. (1902). *Human nature and the social order.* New York: Scribner.

Coopersmith, S. (1967). *The antecedents of self-esteem.* San Francisco: Freeman.

Covington, M. V. (1992). *Making the grade: A self-worth perspective on motivation and school reform.* Cambridge, UK: Cambridge University Press.

Csikszentmihalyi, M. (1990). *Flow: The psychology of optimal experience.* New York: Harper & Row.

Curtis, J., & Altmann, H. (1977). The relationship between teachers' self-concept and the self-concept of students. *Child Study Journal, 7*(1), 17-26.

Darling-Hammond, L. (1997). *The right to learn: A blueprint for school reform*. San Francisco: Jossey-Bass.

Day, C. (1937). *Life with father*. New York: Knopf.

Deci, E. L. (1980). *The psychology of self-determination*. Lexington, MA: Lexington Books.

Deci, R. M., & Ryan, R. M. (1987). *Intrinsic motivation and self-determination in human behavior*. New York: Plenum.

Descartes, R. (1912). *Principles of philosophy: A discourse on method*. New York: E. P. Dutton. (Original work published in 1644)

Diggory, J. C. (1966). *Self-evaluations: Concepts and studies*. New York: John Wiley.

Dworkin, A. G., Haney, C. A., Dworkin, R. J., & Telschow, R. L. (1990, February). Stress and illness behavior among urban public school teachers. *Educational Administration Quarterly, 26*(1), 60-72.

Ellis, A. (1958). Rational psychotherapy. *The Journal of General Psychology, 58*, 35-49.

Ellis, A. (1962). *Reason and emotion in psychotherapy*. New York: Lyle Stuart.

Ellis, A. (1979). Rational-emotive therapy. In R. Corsini (Ed.), *Current psychotherapies* (2nd ed., pp. 185-229). Itasca, IL: Peacock.

Epstein, J. (Ed.). (1981). *Masters: Portraits of great teachers*. New York: Basic Books.

Erikson, E. H. (1963). *Childhood and society* (2nd. ed.). New York: Norton.

Erikson, E. H. (1968). *Identity: Youth and crisis*. New York: Norton.

Freud, A. (1946). *The ego and the mechanisms of defense*. New York: International Universities Press.

Freud, S. (1923). The ego and the id. In *The standard edition of the complete psychological works of Sigmund Freud* (Vol. 19, pp. 3-63). London: Hogarth and the Institute of Psychoanalysis.

Freud, S. (1938). *An outline of psychoanalysis*. New York: Norton.

Freud, S. (1962). The interpretation of dreams. In *The standard edition of the complete psychological works of Sigmund Freud* (Vol. 5, pp. 339-627). London: Hogarth and the Institute of Psychoanalysis. (Original work published in 1900)

Garbarino, J. (1999). *Lost boys: Why our sons turn violent and how we can save them*. New York: Free Press.

Garcia, T., & Pintrich, P. R. (1994). Regulating motivation and cognition in the classroom: The role of self-schemas and self-regulatory strategies. In D. Schunk & B. Zimmerman (Eds.), *Self-regulation of learning and performance: Issues and educational applications* (pp. 127-154). Hillsdale, NJ: Erlbaum.

Garcia Marquez, G. (1988). *Love in the time of cholera*. New York: Alfred A. Knopf.

Gladding, S. T. (1992). *Counseling: A comprehensive profession* (2nd ed.). New York: Merrill.

Glasser, W. (1997). A new look at school failure and success. *Phi Delta Kappan, 78*, 596-602.

Glock, M. D. (1972). Is there a Pygmalion in the classroom? *The Reading Teacher, 25*, 405-408.

Goffin, S. (1989). How well do we respect the children in our care? *Childhood Education, 66*(2), 68-74.

Goldstein, K. (1939). *The organism*. New York: American Book.

Good, T. L. (1981). Teacher expectations and student perceptions: A decade of research. *Educational Leadership, 38*(5), 415-422.

Good, T. L., & Brophy, J. E. (1994). *Looking in classrooms* (6th. ed.). New York: HarperCollins.

Graham, S., & Weiner, B. (1996). Theories and principles of motivation. In D. C. Berliner & C. Calfee (Eds.), *Handbook of Educational Psychology* (pp. 63-84). New York: Macmillan.

Greenberg, L. S., Rice, L. N., & Elliott, R. (1993). *Facilitating emotional change: The moment-by-moment process*. New York: Guilford.

Grinder, J., & Bandler, R. (1981). *Transformations: Neuro-linguistic programming and the structure of hypnosis*. Moab, UT: Real People Press.

Haberman, M. (1995). *Star teachers of children in poverty*. West Lafayette, IN: Kappa Delta Pi.

Hamachek, D. (1994). Changes in the self from a developmental/psychosocial perspective. In T. M. Brinthaupt & R. P. Lipka (Eds.), *Changing the self: Philosophies, techniques, and experiences* (pp. 21-68). Albany: State University of New York Press.

Hansen, J. M., & Childs, J. (1998, September). Creating a school where people like to be. *Educational Leadership*, 14-17.

Harper, K., & Purkey, W. W. (1993). Self-concept-as-learner of middle level students. *National Middle School Journal, 17*(1), 79-87.

Harter, S. (1992). The relationship between perceived competence, affect, and motivational orientation within the classroom: Processes and patterns of change. In A. K. Boggiano & T. S. Pittman (Eds.), *Achievement and motivation: A social-developmental perspective* (pp. 77-114). Cambridge, UK: Cambridge University Press.

Hartman, L. M., & Blankstein, K. R. (Eds.). (1986). *Perception of self in emotional disorder and psychotherapy*. New York: Plenum.

Hattie, J. (1992). *Self-concept*. Hillsdale, NJ: Lawrence Erlbaum.

Hattie, J. (1996, April). *Future directions in self-concept research.* Paper presented at the annual meeting of the American Educational Research Association, New York, NY.

Hayakawa, S. I. (1990). *Language in thought and action* (5th ed.). Washington, DC: Harcourt, Brace & Jovanovich.

Helmstetter, S. (1986). *What to say when you talk to yourself: The major new breakthrough to managing people, yourself, and success.* Scottsdale, AZ: Grendle.

Hilgard, E. R. (1949). Human motives and the concept of the self. *American Psychologist, 4,* 374-382.

Hobbs, N. (Ed.). (1975). *The future of children: Categories, labels, and their consequences.* Nashville, TN: Vanderbilt University Press.

Holdstock, T. L. (1993). Can we afford not to revision the person-centered concept of self? In B. Brazier (Ed.), *Beyond Carl Rogers* (pp. 229-252). London: Constable.

Holdstock, T. L. (1994, September). *Implications of cultural concepts of the self for mental health, mental illness and psychotherapy.* Paper presented at the 16th International Congress of Psychotherapy, Seoul, Korea.

Hull, J. G., & Young, R. D. (1983). The self-awareness reducing effects of alcohol: Evidence and implications. In J. Suls & A. Greenwald (Eds.), *Psychological perspectives on the self* (Vol. 2.). Hillsdale, NJ: Erlbaum.

Insel, P., & Jacobson, L. (1975). *What do you expect? An inquiry into self-fulfilling prophecies.* Menlo Park, CA: Cummings.

Ivey, A. (1977). Cultural expertise: Toward systematic outcome criteria in counseling and psychological education. *Personnel and Guidance Journal, 55,* 296-302.

James, W. (1890). *Principles of psychology* (2 Vols.). Magnolia, MA: Peter Smith.

Jones, S. C., & Panitch, D. (1971). The self-fulling prophecy and interpersonal attraction. *Journal of Experimental Social Psychology, 7,* 356-366.

Jourard, S. M. (1964). *The transparent self: Self-disclosure and well-being.* Princeton, NJ: Van Nostrand.

Jourard, S. M. (1968). *Disclosing man to himself.* Princeton, NJ: Van Nostrand.

Jourard, S. M. (1971). *Self-disclosure: An experimental analysis of the transparent self.* New York: John Wiley.

Kaplan, H. B. (1980). *Deviant behavior in defense of self.* New York: Academic Press.

Kesey, K. (1962). *One flew over the cuckoo's nest.* New York: Viking.

Kiecolt-Glaser, J. K., Garner, W., Speicher, C., Penn, G. M., Holliday, J., & Glasser, R. (1984a). Psychosocial modifiers of immunocompetence in medical students. *Psychosomatic Medicine, 46,* 7-14.

Kiecolt-Glaser, J. K., Ricker, D., Messick, G., Speicher, C. E., Garner, W., & Glasser, R. (1984b). Urinary cortisol, cellular immunocompetency and loneliness in psychiatric inpatients. *Psychosomatic Medicine, 46,* 15-24.

Kohn, A. (1994, December). The truth about self-esteem. *Phi Delta Kappan,* 272-283.

Kruglanski, A., Stein, C., & Ritter, A. (1977). Contingencies of exogenous reward and task performance: On the minimax strategy in instrumental behavior. *Journal of Applied Social Psychology, 60,* 141-148.

Landried, S. (1989). "Enabling" undermines responsibility in students. *Educational Leadership, 47*(3), 79-83.

Lecky, P. (1945). *Self-consistency: A theory of personality.* New York: Island.

L'Ecuyer, R. (1992). An experiential-developmental framework and methodology to study the transformations of the self-concept from infancy to old age. In T. M. Brinthaupt & R.P. Lipka (Eds.), *The self: Definitional and methodological issues* (pp. 96-134). Albany: State University of New York Press.

Lepper, M. R., & Hodell, M. (1989). Intrinsic motivation in the classroom. In C. Ames & R. Ames (Eds.), *Motivation in education* (pp. 73-106). San Diego, CA: Academic Press.

Lewin, K. (1935). *A dynamic theory of personality.* New York: McGraw-Hill.

Loftus, E. (1980). *Memory: Surprising new insights into how we remember and why we forget.* Reading, MA: Addison-Wesley.

Lowry, H. F. (1961, March). *The mouse and Henry Carson.* Opening address, Conference on Outstanding Students in Liberal Arts Colleges, Buck Hill Falls, PA.

Mahler, M. S. (1979). *The selected papers of Margaret Mahler* (Vols. 1-2). New York: Jason Aronson.

Mahoney, M. J. (Ed.). (1995). *Cognitive and constructive psychotherapies: Theory, research, and practice.* Washington, DC: Springer and the American Psychological Association.

Marcia, J. E. (1987). The identity status approach to the study of ego identity development. In T. Honess & K. Yardley (Eds.), *Self and identity: Perspectives across the lifespan.* London: Routledge & Kegan Paul.

Marcia, J. E. (1991). Identity and self-development. In R. M. Lerner, A. C. Peterson, & J. Brooks-Gunn (Eds.), *Encyclopedia of adolescence* (Vol 1). New York: Garland.

Markus, H., Cross, S., & Wurf, E. (1990). The role of the self-system in competence. In R. Sternberg & J. Kolligian (Eds.), *Competence considered* (pp. 205-225). New Haven, CT: Yale University Press.

Markus, H., & Nurius, P. (1986). Possible selves. *American Psychologist, 41*(9), 954-969.

Markus, H., & Wurf, E. (1987). The dynamic self-concept: A social psychological analysis. In M. Rosenzweig & L. Porter (Eds.), *Annual Review of Psychology,* (Vol. 48, pp. 299-338). Palo Alto, CA: Annual Reviews.

Marsh, H. W. (1989). Age and sex effects in multiple dimensions of self-concept. *Journal of Educational Psychology, 81,* 417-430.

Marsh, H. W. (1993). The multidimensional structure of academic self-concept: Invariance over gender and age. *American Educational Research Journal, 30,* 841-860.

Maslow, A. H. (1954). *Motivation and personality.* New York: Harper & Row.

Matthews, D. B. (1991). The effects of school environment on intrinsic motivation of middle school children. *Journal of Humanistic Education and Development, 30,* 30-36.

Maugham, W. S. (1944). *The razor's edge.* New York: Doubleday.

Maultsby, M. C., Jr. (1975). *Help yourself to happiness.* Boston: Herman.

Maultsby, M. C., Jr. (1977). The ABC's of better emotional self-control. In C. Zastrow & D. Chang, (Eds.), *The personal problem solver* (pp. 3-18). Englewood Cliffs, NJ: Prentice Hall.

May, R. (1969). *Love and will.* New York: Norton.

McCaslin, M., & Good, T. L. (1992). Complaint cognition: The misalliance of management and instructional goals in current school reform. *Educational Researcher, 21*(3), 4-17.

McMillan, J. H. (1980). Enhancing self-concepts of junior high school students. *The Humanist Educator, 18,* 4.

Mead, G. H. (1934). *Mind, self and society.* Chicago: University of Chicago Press.

Meichenbaum, D. (1977). *Cognitive-behavior modification: An integrative approach.* New York: Plenum.

Meichenbaum, D. (1985). *Stress inoculation training.* New York: Pergamon.

Millay, E. S. V. (1949). *Collected poems.* New York: Harper & Brothers.

Milne, A. A. (1926). *Winnie-The-Pooh.* New York: E. P. Dutton.

Montmayor, R., & Eisen, M. (1977). The development of self-conceptions from childhood to adolescence. *Developmental Psychology, 13,* 314-319.

Moore, W., & Esselman, M. (1992, April). *Teacher efficacy, power, school climate and achievement: A desegregating district's experience.* Paper presented at Annual Meeting of the American Educational Research Association, San Francisco, CA.

Neumann, A. (1995). Context, cognition, and culture: A case analysis of collegiate leadership and cultural change. *American Educational Research Journal, 32*(2), 251-279.

Nisbett, R. E., & Ross, L. D. (1980). *Human inference: Strategies and shortcomings of social judgment.* Englewood Cliffs, NJ: Prentice Hall.

Noddings, N. (1984). *Caring: A feminine approach to ethics and moral education.* Berkeley: University of California Press.

Noddings, N. (1992). *The challenge to care in schools.* New York: Teachers College Press.

Noddings, N. (1993). *Educating for intelligent belief or unbelief.* New York: Columbia University and Teachers College Press.

Nutt-Williams, E., & Hill, C. E. (1996). The relationship between self-talk and therapy process variables for novice therapists. *Journal of Counseling Psychology, 43,* 170-177.

Oberg, A. (1987). The ground of professional practice. In J. Lowyck (Ed.), *Teacher thinking and professional action.* Lisse: Swets & Zeitlinger.

Pajares, M. F. (1992). Teachers' beliefs and educational research: Cleaning up a messy construct. *Review of Educational Research, 62*(3), 307-332.

Palmer, P. J. (1997, November/December). The heart of a teacher: Identity and integrity in teaching. *Change,* 15-21.

Posner, G. J., Strike, J. A., Hewson, P. W., & Gertzog, W. A. (1982). Accommodation of a scientific conception: Toward a theory of conceptual change. *Science Education, 66,* 211-227.

Purkey, W. W. (1970). *Self concept and school achievement.* Englewood Cliffs, NJ: Prentice Hall.

Purkey, W. W., Cage, B., & Graves, W. H. (1973). The Florida Key: A scale to infer learner self-concept. *Journal of Educational and Psychological Measurement, 33,* 979-984.

Purkey, W. W., & Novak, J. M. (1996). *Inviting school success: A self-concept approach to teaching, learning, and democratic practice* (3rd ed.). Belmont, CA: Wadsworth.

Purkey, W. W., & Schmidt, J. J. (1996). *Invitational counseling: A self-concept approach to professional practice.* Pacific Grove, CA: Brooks/Cole.

Purkey, W. W., & Stanley, P. H. (1990). A blue and orange card metaphor for counselors. *Journal of Counseling and Development, 68,* 587-588.

Purkey, W. W., & Stanley, P. H. (1997). *The inviting school treasury: 1001 ways to invite student success.* Greenville, NC: Brookcliff.

Raimy, V. C. (1948). Self-reference in counseling interviews. *Journal of Consulting Psychology, 12,* 153-163.

Rogers, C. R. (1951). *Client-centered therapy.* Boston: Houghton Mifflin.

Rogers, C. R. (1959). *Counseling and psychotherapy: Theory and practice.* New York: Harper & Row.

Rogers, C. R. (1969). *Freedom to learn.* Columbus, OH: Merrill.

Rogers, C. (1974). In retrospect: Forty-six years. *American Psychologist, 29,* 115.

Rosenthal, R., & Jacobson, L. (1968). *Pygmalion in the classroom: Teacher expectation and pupils' intellectual development.* New York: Holt, Rinehart & Winston.

Ross, J. A. (1998). Antecedents and consequences of teacher efficacy. In J. Brophy (Ed.), *Advances in research on teaching* (Vol. 7, pp. 49-74). Greenwich, CT: JAI.

Scheier, M. F., & Carver, C. S. (1993). On the power of positive thinking: The benefits of being optimistic. *Current Directions in Psychological Science, 1,* 26-30.

Schmidt, J. J., Shields, C. W., & Ciechalski, J. C. (1998). The Inviting-Disinviting Index: A study of validity and reliability. *Journal of Invitational Theory and Practice, 5*(1), 31-42.

Schunk, D. H. (1984). The self-efficacy perceptive on achievement behavior. *Educational Psychologist, 19,* 199-218.

Schunk, D. H. (1989). Social cognitive therapy and self-regulating learning. In B. J. Zimmerman & D. H. Schunk (Eds.), *Self-regulated and academic achievement: Theory, research, and practice* (pp. 83-110). New York: Springer Verlag.

Schunk, D. H. (1990). Goal setting and self-efficacy during self-regulated learning. *Educational Psychologist, 25,* 70-86.

Schunk, D., & Zimmerman, B. (1994). (Eds.). *Self-regulation of learning and performance: Issues and educational applications.* Hillsdale, NJ: Erlbaum.

Seeman, J. (1988). The rediscovery of the self in American psychology. *Person-Centered Review, 3,* 145-165.

Seligman, M. E. (1975). *Helplessness: On depression, and death.* San Francisco: Freeman.

Seligman, M. E. (1990). *Learned optimism.* New York: Knopf.

Sergiovanni, T. J. (1994). *Building community in schools.* San Francisco: Jossey-Bass.

Short, P., & Short, R. (1988). Perceived classroom environment of student behavior in secondary schools. *Educational Research Quarterly, 12,* 35-39.

Snow, R. E., Corno, L., & Jackson, D., III. (1996). Individual differences in affective and cognitive functions. In D. C. Berliner & R. C. Calfee (Eds.), *Handbook of educational psychology* (pp. 243-310). New York: Macmillan.

Snygg, D., & Combs, A. W. (1949). *Individual behavior.* Harper & Row.

Sokolov, A. N. (1972). *Inner speech and thought.* New York: Plenum.

Stanley, P. H., & Purkey, W. W. (1994). Student self-concept-as-learner: Does invitational education make a difference? *Research in the Schools, 1*(2), 15-22.

Steele, C. M. (1988). The psychology of self-affirmation: Sustaining the integrity of the self. *Advances in Experimental Social Psychology, 21,* 261-302.

Steele, C. M., & Liu, T. J. (1983). Dissonance processes as self-affirmation. *Journal of Personality and Social Psychology, 45,* 5-19.

Strahan, D. (1990). From seminars to lessons: A middle school language arts teacher's reflections on instructional improvement. *Journal of Curriculum Studies, 22,* 233-251.

Stipek, D., & MacIver, D. (1989). Developmental change in children's' assessments of intellectual competence. *Child Development, 60,* 521-538.

Toombs, S. K. (1994). Disability and the self. In T. M. Brinthaupt & R. P. Lipka (Eds.), *Changing the self: Philosophies, techniques, and experiences* (pp. 337-357). Albany: State University of New York Press.

Tschannen-Moran, M., Hoy, A. W., & Hoy, W. K. (1998). Teacher efficacy: Its meaning and measure. *Review of Educational Research, 68*(2), 202-248.

Vygotsky, L. S. (1935/1978). *Mind in society: The development of higher psychological processes.* Cambridge, MA: Harvard University Press.

Vygotsky, L. S. (1962). *Thought and language.* Cambridge, MA: MIT Press.

Watson, D. L., & Tharp, R. G. (1989). *Self-directed behavior: Self-modification for personal adjustment.* Pacific Grove, CA: Brooks/Cole.

Watson, J. B. (1925). *Behaviorism.* New York: Norton & Company.

Weinberg, C. (1989, Fall). Teachers against stress: Rethinking beliefs about teaching. *Teacher Education Quarterly, 73-84.*

Whitman, W. (1948). From *The complete poetry and prose of Walt Whitman as prepared for the death-bed edition.* New York: Pellegrini & Cudahy.

Wiemer, D. D., & Purkey, W. W. (1994). Love thyself as thy neighbor? Self-other orientations of inviting behaviors. *Journal of Invitational Theory and Practice, 3*(1), 25-33.

Wiggins, J. D., & Giles, T. A. (1984). The relationship between counselors' and students self-esteem as related to counseling outcomes. *The School Counselor, 32,* 18-22.

Zastrow, C. (1979). *Talk to yourself: Use the power of self talk.* Englewood Cliffs, NJ: Prentice Hall.

Zastrow, C. (1994). Conceptualizing and changing the self from a rational therapy perspective. In T. M. Brinthaupt & R. P. Lipka (Eds.), *Changing the self: Philosophies, techniques, and experiences* (pp. 175-199). Albany: State University of New York Press.

Zimmerman, B. J., Bandura, A., & Martinez-Pons, M. (1992). Self-motivation for academic attainment: The role of self-efficacy beliefs and personal goal setting. *American Educational Research Journal, 29,* 663-676.

Zimmerman, I. L., & Allebrand, G. N. (1965). Personality characteristics and attitudes toward achievement of good and poor readers. *Journal of Educational Research, 59,* 28-30.

Index

CORWIN
PRESS

The Corwin Press logo—a raven striding across an open book—
represents the happy union of courage and learning. We are a
professional-level publisher of books and journals for K–12 educators, and we are committed to creating and providing resources that
embody these qualities. Corwin's motto is "Success for All Learners."